Screwtape Writes Again

Screwtape
Writes Again

Walter
Martin

VISION HOUSE PUBLISHERS
Santa Ana, California 92705

Dedication

To the memory of C. S. Lewis,
a dedicated Christian apologist and evangelist,
who made insight into the Satanic realm a vital
practiced study.

"He being dead still speaks" (Hebrews 11:4).

*I saw Satan fall like lightning from heaven. ...
The devil comes down to you, having great wrath,
because he knows that his time is short.*

— Luke 10:18; Revelation 12:12

PREFACE

Since the greatly lamented passing of counter agent "L," whose magnificent deciphering of the infernal code 666 was so instrumental in multiplying our knowledge of the methods of DDI°, much new data has been intercepted and patiently accumulated.

After many laborious years spent in research and with the help of "L's" various observations and expertise, I have at last managed to penetrate still another code, which for reasons of security we will refer to only in passing. The method of interception we are, of course, not at liberty to discuss, but suffice it to say that the information is of paramount importance, since it contains detailed correspondence from His Abysmal Sublimity, Undersecretary Screwtape, T.E., B.S., that most remarkable Supervisor of Temptational Tactics, whose writings have shed so much light, albeit inadvertently, on the Kingdom below.

As always, a note of caution must be voiced. Screwtape, as "L" pointed out, is a habitual liar about certain details, particularly in the area of motivation, self-criticism, and Christian conduct. However, there is every reason for believing that his instructions to Wormwood contained herein were intended to fortify him for "front-line" combat against the human race. In a number of instances, it checks out remarkably well with certain facts in our own Master Training Manual (O.T.—N.T. 1-66).

It must also be remembered that some expressions and arguments of Screwtape will seem so familiar to many that

---

° *Department of Devilish Intelligence*

they may be tempted to concur with his conclusions without examining the premises. Never forget Screwtape's maxim for all young fiends in basic training to become tempters: "If you can't convince them, then confuse them —the next best thing to a damned soul is a neutralized Christian!" With the sincere hope that these translations will prove as profitable to a new generation seeking protective knowledge of the Unholy as agent "L's" were to his contemporaries, this additional correspondence is now published.

Letter I

My Dear Wormwood:

I address you once again now that the unpleasantness of my recent trial on charges of "ineptness and negligence" is behind us. Despite my harsh language regarding your failure to salvage your former patient from the Enemy, you know I have always considered you one of my best tempters and favorite nephews. Surely you must have guessed I was only joking when I spoke of my ravenous appetite and described you as a tasty morsel! Who could have foreseen that you would take my harmless criticism of your last assignment on such a personal level? I assure you I was not aware that you numbered among your relatives the illustrious and dread Dragonslik (Exalted Director of Devilish Intelligence). I must also congratulate you on the presentation of your case before the Hades High Court, particularly your appeal to our Father's standard of excellence for all senior as well as junior tempters.

I confess I quite underestimated your persuasive abilities and must admit that you conducted yourself on the whole as a mature and seasoned fiend. I do feel, however, that some of your remarks were ill-conceived and slanted, particularly when I was described as a "square, semisenile devil of the old school" and as one who "obstructs the development of young devils by his inept and dated tutoring." On the basis of my long service record, however, the whole matter has now been resolved with my acquittal and you have been reassigned, as you know, to my charge.

Assisting you with your new patient will be Legion, a seasoned campaigner who has had extensive encounters with the Enemy during his earthly sojourn and is an experienced tempter. Feel free to consult with him at any time, but remember, you must report directly to me, and believe me, I shall be keeping close tabs on your performance record! All the relatives in hell will not help you to escape this time if you fail or bungle it! But let's not dwell on these things. We shall, instead, proceed to the condition of your new patient.

As you have probably observed, he is a product of what is currently known as the "now" generation. This allegedly new breed of humans is characterized by impatience, contempt for history and older values, and a desire for instant solutions to complex and, at times, impossible problems. We have found it to our advantage to encourage these traits, particularly the so-called antiestablishment ethic that permeates all of them. Impress upon your patient an emotional attitude of reaction to abuses he sees in society, rather than thinking through the cause and possible remedies for them. He must be led to think that his parents' generation is responsible for all the imperfections he discerns, and that his generation must "put right" all the problems "they" created. Don't let him catch a glimpse of the obvious fact that *we* are largely responsible for the ills of mankind by seducing them to disobey the Enemy's law. Keep him constantly blaming others for the condition of the world and he will become just another sacrifice upon the altar of the great god "Now." He must not discover that the Enemy created order in society and that the "establishment" so far as it conforms to that order represents the Enemy's kingdom. His real rebellion is, therefore, not as much against society as it is against the Enemy, something your patient would certainly not admit. From this position, it is only one step to pushing him into anarchy. Across the centuries we have made great use of the concept of anarchy, particularly among the disenchanted and the blindly idealistic.

What they never seem to learn is that anarchy, by definition, is lawlessness and disorganization. Yet the moment one unites with others to promote its aims, one becomes organized and ceases to be anarchist. If they ever learn that, for all their bleating about the abuses of society, they have no real program to replace it except practices which, historically, have plunged all societies foolish enough to embrace them into impotence and despair.

The Enemy well knows our tactics in this area, however, and the church is his answer to them. Through the church the Enemy's Spirit unifies them and forms the spiritual mortar that can hold together any society that recognizes and practices His law.

So then, dear Wormwood, keep your patient thinking only about "now"—seldom about the past and never about the future. Any issue that is new and "now," whether religious, moral, ethical, or political, is preferable to his discovering his spiritual bankruptcy and thereby possibly falling victim to the agents of heaven and the unity of the church. I know you will pursue this area successfully, keeping always in mind the infernal motto of our Father below— "to hell with everybody."

Your affectionate uncle,
SCREWTAPE

Letter II

My Dear Wormwood:

I was somewhat surprised, to say the least, that you have not encouraged your patient to read more religious literature, particularly the so-called "modern theologians," who are philosophically oriented. Some of our greatest triumphs have been in this line of endeavor due to the fact that humans love complexity of thought. This they pursue on the totally baseless assumption that complexity indicates profundity or truth. Steer your patient, therefore, to those writers whose content is limited but who "sound good" or "read well" or "write relevantly"—three meaningless traits when separated from spiritual reality. Such writers are marvelously adept at the manipulation of the Enemy's basic vocabulary and can sound for all the world like His servants, while at heart doubting or outright just not believing what He has said. Nothing will upset your patient more than to be taught what are really *our* views in the Enemy's name and by someone "ordained" in His service. In the most pious terms we have seen to it that they correctly redefine His gospel out of existence (the Alice in Wonderland approach) and deny His authority and redemptive intentions as well as His appearance as a human. What a delight to hell to observe such faithful service to our cause!

Channel your patient's thoughts in the prideful notion that he is more advanced than his fellows because he "reads the great contemporary minds" and is not "narrow" in his concepts of religion.

From what you tell me there is little risk that the clergyman he now listens to during his sporadic attendance at church will lead him anywhere near the Enemy, since the clergyman is also a devotee of the "new theology." His last Easter sermon on the Resurrection (according to Legion's report) reveals that he has become most astute at what we have come to regard here in hell as the "Watergate syndrome." When in doubt, redefine!

He succeeded in rambling for some forty minutes, mouthing the correct cliches but actually milking the Enemy's message dry of all real content or meaning. When he finished there was no resurrection—only "something of great import" which in some vague way related to the welfare of humanity. It ranked favorably with his Christmas message, which amounted to little more than the fatherhood of God, the brotherhood of man, and the neighborhood of Bethlehem! Now in all this I hope you will discern what many young tempters are prone to forget. Always emphasize the word "new," as in "new morality," "new theology," "new situation ethics," etc., since humans gravitate toward anything that appears to be new, though as we know (and hell knows they should have learned by now!) there is "no new thing under the sun." We are always dealing with old information brightly garbed in the trappings of each new culture or successive civilization. They must not ever guess in our Father's couplet that "old error in new dress is ever error nonetheless." It is evident to any thinking person that truth never becomes truer with the passage of time, since by its very nature truth is unalterable.

But that is another subject for another time. We have encouraged such clergymen to gouge from the Enemy's Training Manual what is in reality "another Jesus," a different spirit (to be sure!), and another gospel. Added to this formidable counterfeiting, we have promulgated false apostles and ministers, thus redefining the entire so-called "sacred" vocabulary of the Enemy's gospel and thereby reducing it to a shambles of euphemistic, meaningless trivia. What matter to us if they use holy names and titles so long as we can reduce them to a semantic jungle of religious confusion? Thanks to such modern ministers and writers, our counterfeits have replaced the genuine and we continue to perpetuate the grand illusion that all this is angelic light. Be careful, however, that your patient does not discover that where there is a counterfeit there also exists an original! Never allow him to define a term in context or actually ask whether such modern thinkers represent the Enemy's historic intentions. For example, he must be prevented from realizing that if all that Christianity can claim for the Enemy's Resurrection is the triumph of spirit over flesh, then certainly no more can be claimed for Him than for any other good man—survival of the spirit after death. *We* know all too well what the word "resurrection" means, but your patient must not be permitted to know, for without this knowledge he will never understand the Enemy's plan. This, then, is the true value of theological term-switching. It permits us to copy the Enemy's message and lull our patients to semantic slumber—a sleep that knows only the awakening of hell!

I applaud your observation that you must keep your patient's minister forever on the frail fence of indecision. Be sure he never really chooses the Enemy's side; keep him fearful of rejection by his sophisticated peers or rebellion by some militant members of his congregation. Have him speak "fearlessly" on issues generally agreed upon as "relevant to the human dilemma" (a most useful catchall term!) and have him accept the praise of others as proof that he has spoken decisively. Such phrases as "truth is progressive" and "the light gets brighter" are most useful here just so long as he does not learn, as we have already observed, that truth cannot become truer, though light may in some instances tend to get brighter. By such tactics your patient will soon be on the same theological fence with his clergyman, and the Enemy's will can be even more obscured in the hazy maze of modern scholarship and "enlightened" double-talk.

If your patient should become suspicious of your efforts in this area, press home the idea that true religion is "doing for others" despite doctrinal differences; underline the Enemy's so-called "love" at the expense of His final justice. In this way he will come to think that the Enemy will excuse his willful lack of obedience because of "love," thereby most certainly courting His justice. By all that's unholy, what irony! The Enemy's justice must ultimately send your patient to us, because in the name of His love we will have obscured your patient's view of His justice!

We have much, then, for which to thank so-called "liberal theology" and clergymen. They are the real rascals of every generation; as someone has said, "the shame of heaven, the joy of hell—the preacher's on the fence!"

To your last question I must answer an emphatic yes. Philosophical theology can be of considerable use to us in misdirecting your patient's thoughts. We have despoiled many a mind through secular philosophy and empty intellectual conceit, for, as one noted enemy of ours once put it, "There can be no agreement between Athens and Jerusalem." The former is symbolic of the virtual deification and worship of human wisdom, the latter of submission to the Enemy. Mind that you do not get him into too much speculation about the problem of evil, lest the contrast provoke his curiosity and he begin to seriously consider the Enemy's claims. Do not put him in contact with Christian philosophers, for they sometimes correctly appraise our aims and techniques, with dangerous consequences.

One of them recently risked the wrath of hell by suggesting that our Father's exit from the upper kingdom was due to his pride and the Enemy's judgment. This is, of course, a vile slander given some credence by its repetition in the Enemy's Training Manual (O.T., Vol. 23, Ch. 14:12).

Actually, our Father made a logistically brilliant withdrawal from the Enemy's presence and then penetrated His creation on all levels with a disruptive fury that cursed nature itself and brought death and destruction to the Enemy's Edenic paradise.

Our Father below is the real victor and will sustain that victory with his eventual conquest of the cosmos and enthronement as the archetypal antiestablishment hero. It was he who championed the cause of celestial democracy and self-determination in the face of the Enemy's demagogic attempt to enforce His obnoxious will upon creation.

We now know the Enemy's claim to omnipotence to be purely propaganda, for, as Devilish Intelligence has observed, He would long ago have annihilated our forces if this were true. Quite properly, our Father will not crawl back through the accursed gates of pearl murmuring any penitent Magnificat, as some misled humans have suggested. Contrary to the malicious slanders of the Enemy, our Father's alleged fall was actually a great step forward toward his inevitable divinity. The Enemy has conceded already that our Father is "the god of this age" and "the god of this world," which is the handwriting on the wall and ought to settle the matter. Our Father is not, as your research questionnaire reflects, a "self-deceived cosmic paranoid" suffering from "delusions of grandeur" and "hallucinations of heaven." Don't ever let me catch you even thinking, much less repeating, such unspeakably degenerate and vile accusations against our Father even in the interest of what you term "field research." Furthermore, you contemptible little. . . .

(At this point the manuscript breaks off and is resumed in a different hand.)

Due to the extremely provocative nature of your inquiries, Undersecretary Screwtape has been overtaken by an uncontrollable fit of rage suffered by His Excellency in the line of duty. He has temporarily assumed the form of what appears to be a rather large red jellyfish and has set about ravenously nibbling on some unfortunate new arrivals from earth.

Regrettably but diabolically yours,
TOADPIPE,

For His Abysmal Sublimity, Undersecretary Screwtape, T.E.

Letter III

My Dear Wormwood:

Your last letter disturbed me terribly, and I feel that it is necessary for me to convey to you in the strongest possible terms my feelings as of this writing.

The conversion to Christianity of your patient cannot be taken lightly by any standards of hell. You simply must recognize that your prime responsibility as a tempter is first and foremost to prevent such events from ever occurring and, secondly, if they occur, to do all that is possible to pluck the seed of your patient's newfound faith from the soil of his soul so that it does not take root. Since you have obviously failed in the first part, we must now direct our attention and efforts toward your success in the second part. Please do not think that I have forgotten your first misadventure in this area. We keep extensive records here, as you know. So despite your considerable influence with Dragonslik and other high-ranking relatives in the hierarchy, this regretful ineptitude on your part will cost you. Believe me, you will pay for it! Let us address ourselves, however, more negatively, to the reclamation of your patient's soul, confident as always that our Father below has the necessary experience and background to rescue him from that great misnomer, the Enemy's "love."

Your patient is being exposed for the first time to Christian fellowship both in the church he now attends regularly and in the company of new friends he has made there. Be sure to bring him in contact with the extremely pious variety of church member who has a reputation (preferably undeserved) for "spirituality" and "maturity." Assist him whenever possible to think of his fellow Christians as shining examples of "what a Christian should be like." Constantly remind him that Christians should be "perfect" and that his minister should be a flawless saint right out of the book of martyrs. Never let him suspect that perfection or "completion," as the Enemy terms it, is the result of a lifetime of spiritual growth and that there are no instant saints, though it serves our ends to cultivate that illusion.

This will all prove worthwhile when he observes that his pastor and the other examples of spirituality he has been admiring have all the failings of the flesh which he possesses, hopefully even more! He will then become disappointed and discouraged and start casting about for some explanation, which is just the right moment to stimulate his pride. Give him the suggestion that he isn't really so bad after all—in fact a good deal better than those he once idolized—and it won't be long before he is so taken up with such comparisons that the real meaning of the church as a fellowship of worshippers will be obscured.

As long as we can keep Christians making comparisons between themselves and judging one another on that basis, we cloud the fact that the Enemy wishes them to compare themselves only to Him, so that one standard judges all. This has been the remarkably successful purpose of his so-called "law." Through it He reveals that all humans are transgressors and in need (so He affirms) of His forgiveness. Of course this is all rank absurdity, for, as our Father has declared, we do not need His forgiveness or miserly gifts. We shall do without them, and it is our task to see that humans do without them also. Such comparisons go a long way toward realizing that goal.

Try, if at all possible, to have your patient tramp from church to church in quest of some "new" experience, "greater" speaker, or "better" Christians with whom to compare himself. You are quite right in noting that this is not the fault of the church but of his own immaturity and pride. But this will keep him from supporting his local congregation (which, according to our Father below, is the infantry of the Enemy's army) and will prevent him from sinking any roots into that all-too-fertile ground of fellowship with other Christians. If he does elect to stay in his present church, seize every opportunity to have his fellow Christians like him, respect him, and then propose him for the office of elder, deacon, vestryman, etc.

The less he knows about spiritual things, the more we can use him in a position of influence to disrupt the pastor and those who are more mature in the Enemy's service. Persuade them to ordain him quickly to his new responsibilities, and persuade him to accept even though he is "unworthy." It is positively amazing how false humility can be utilized at this juncture most successfully. Christians never seem to learn (and that to our advantage, I might add) that the pastor should choose and ordain those best qualified to assist him in congregational tasks, since he is obviously the best qualified to recognize maturity and ability among his charges. However, by persistent efforts over the centuries we have influenced them to conceive of the church as a democratic society rather than the theocracy the Enemy designed it to be. We must foster this superb error in judgment whenever possible so that they will continue to believe that majority rule is the Enemy's will for them.

Some of them actually hold that 51 percent of the congregation constitutes the very voice of the Enemy—a real stroke of devilish deception they have yet to detect despite centuries of sound advice.

One final note of warning must be sounded here should your patient escape these temptations. There are always hypocrites in the Enemy's camp who act out a role of spirituality while zealously searching about for opportunities to be carnal. See that he meets some of these and notices their inconsistencies. Set him to wondering why the pastor doesn't preach against them and why other Christians do not rebuke them openly. With a little studied effort, you can plant the idea that they are all hypocrites and that he is well rid of the whole lot. What he must not uncover is the truth that it is better for him to spend a little time in church with *some* of the hypocrites than eternity in our Father's house below with *all* of them! Make sure he confuses Christianity with churchianity, the one being the Enemy's pet project, the other a masterful perversion of it. The former has substance as well as form, the latter form without substance. Nothing suits us so well as clergymen, people, and churches that go through the motions of spiritual reality (building programs, services, bazaars, festivals, etc.) while missing the whole point—the worship of the Enemy and "love" for each other. So don't overlook these opportunities. Seize and exploit them.

Your affectionate uncle,
SCREWTAPE

Letter IV

My Dear Wormwood:

From what you tell me in your last letter, your patient has recently discovered the fact that Christians gossip about one another. This is an excellent opportunity to exploit his revulsion at what he considers an appalling practice. Of course he does not as yet realize that becoming a Christian provides no guarantee of perfection on earth, since the Enemy prefers to remake the two-legged vermin in what He calls His own image over the period of their entire lives. Thanks to the untiring and splendid efforts of our Father below, however, we have over the centuries aborted millions of such attempts. At any rate, this all tends to make your patient quick to judge the imperfections of others while he remains blissfully blind to his own.

The history of humanity indicates that experience teaches humans very little; they have not yet learned that gossip inevitably punishes the gossiper as well as harming the victim. Encourage your patient to believe that Christians are the worst gossips of all because "they know better." Make sure that he does not detect the fallacy that, though they may bear the greatest burden of guilt because they know better, that does not necessarily make them the worst offenders in the practice itself. In point of fact, the Enemy appears to have succeeded in progressively reducing their desire to practice such things, and his success is in direct proportion to their growth as Christians.

You see then, Wormwood, how important it is to keep him from maturing spiritually. I am sure you will recall your basic training under Dr. Slubgob at the Tempter's Training College for Young Devils, and the all-important maxim "stunted Christians are sterile Christians." You see, the next best thing to a damned soul is a sterile Christian. If we cannot have their souls (which I do not at all concede!), we *must* succeed in neutralizing them in their spiritual lives so that they cannot "testify" for the Enemy's cause. To that end, make sure that he overhears Christians gossiping and learns to judge all of them by the sins of a select number of offenders. In a recent conversation with Aspnip, Executive Director of the Division of Gossip and Slander (Academy of Satanic Sciences), he reminded me that Satanic slander properly executed is similar to opening a large feather pillow on a front lawn during a high wind. Try as they will, the humans will never get the feathers back in the bag! Since we are the authors and refiners of deception through the ages, the gossiper must *never* understand the impact of his words or that he is really slandering another person's character. Convince him (or her, as the case may be) that they are "only telling the truth" or, better yet, that "it is their Christian duty" to warn of the defects of others.

Some of the most apparently gentle souls to be found in thousands of churches the world over can be transformed by gossiping into our most valued church asset. They would never dream of blasphemy or adultery or idolatry, but through gossip they are guilty of "murder" in the Enemy's eyes and of transgressing that most repugnant of the

Enemy's dictums, "love one another." Be advised that there is of course no such thing as "love" the way the Enemy has defined it, and that at length our Intelligence Division will formulate an analysis and expose of the whole charade. But for now it admittedly remains a mystery to us. Another particularly helpful by-product of promoting gossip in your patient is the generation of carnality or worldliness in those who, under normal circumstances, would shun it at once. It is obvious to all but the most spiritually keen humans that carnality is the willing handmaiden of division, envy, and strife among the Enemy's disciples and should therefore be avoided by them at all costs. However, the tongue of the human can both bless and blaspheme, praise and pester, unify and divide, and it is to our interests to see that anything which will advance our cause is promulgated. We know that the Enemy despises the use of the tongue to sow division among His people. So it is obvious that the patient must not learn this nor the fact that carnal gossip takes many forms.

In one of our most successful cases we persuaded a rather talented, but proud, Christian leader that he could slander other members of the clergy because they were not as "orthodox" as he fancied himself to be. He was a fine speaker and writer, with a growing audience that rapidly multiplied and accepted his "orthodoxy." As time passed he led tens of thousands into an ecclesiastical position that separated his own church and hundreds of others from other Christians, and we were delighted to see untold numbers of his followers despising their churches and ministers and gossiping about their brothers, all in the righteous name of "orthodoxy." Quite honestly, the man's creed wasn't any more orthodox than that of the people he slandered, but how we worked to convince him that it was! Today his church is half-empty; he is separated from and bitter against anyone who disagrees with him. His word is regarded the least by those who know him best. Now *that* is setting the tongue on fire in hell and watching it scorch the earth that one day our Father, not the meek, will inherit! But let us press on to the rest of your letter.

I noticed that you are inordinately occupied with the practice that all young tempters have, namely, that of dangling the sins of *commission* in front of your patient as if these alone were useful. You must put that idea out of your head. Some of the sins that damn men most consistently are not sins of *commission* but sins of *omission*. The road to our Father's house below is best traveled as a gentle incline rather than a steep slope. Some gossip is expertly practiced in this very way. Frequently, active—in fact, overt—gossipers will address passive listeners, some of whom know the falsity of their statements and appeal to them for verification of their gossip. Our task at this juncture is to keep such people from saying anything, so that their silence is interpreted by others as agreement with the gossip, thus adding weight to it. Distract them with thoughts of "not wanting to get involved" or "it's none of my business."

Silence in the presence of such slander causes the person to become an accomplice and makes it easier each time thereafter to obtain the same results with him. Never forget, the Enemy has declared it to be a grievous sin to keep silence in the presence of evil and not to tell the evil-doer his crime and its punishment.° This is of little interest to us except academically, but if we can use His Word to trip and trap His servants so that they at length become the property of our Father, so much the better for us and the worse for them.

Your affectionate uncle,
SCREWTAPE

° *Screwtape doubtless here refers to Ezekiel 33:8.*

Letter V

My Dear Wormwood:

You wasted a great deal of time in your last letter bothering about your patient's daily habit of reading the Enemy's Word. You young tempters have the annoying faculty of taking a teardrop of knowledge and diffusing it into an ocean of empty prattle. When will you learn that *reading* His Word is not the same as *studying* it?

To be sure, we must never encourage them to utilize the Enemy's Training Manual, but if they do desire to study it, you must act quickly. One of our most successful ploys through the centuries has been to equate reading with study and form with content, so that the humans become frustrated and thus come to a totally false conclusion. We should permit them to follow a mechanical 15 or 20 minutes a day of routine perusing of the Enemy's Word, urging them to concentrate upon how much they read rather than on either its meaning or practical application. By your attentive presence at such piously termed "quiet times" or "moments of meditation" you may cause them to become subtly devoid of any real absorption of spiritual truth through the single and simple expediency of combining speed with pride. Keep your patient's mind on covering as many pages as he can while reflecting, subconsciously, upon how much more spiritual he or she is than those of his brothers who conduct their devotions differently than he.

Suggest to him that if he must "read the Word through at least three times a year" (one of our better slogans), speed is of the essence. This is a far better approach than letting him pray as he slowly reads, seeking direction and insight from the Enemy's Spirit. Remember that the Spirit delights in teaching those who pursue this method, those who are truly intent upon drawing near to the Enemy rather than in engaging in the mental and linguistic gymnastics we have substituted. You might have a chat sometimes with Muddlescrounge, who has been busily promulgating speed-reading courses, utilizing the human's reasoning that if it works in business it can work in religion. He has found that his patients respond remarkably well to this type of appeal, to the point where speed-reading has become an end in itself, so that his charges are now so occupied with their new toy of "rapid reading" (and comparing their rates of speed and comprehension) that the Enemy's Manual has become just another challenge to their eye muscles and their brains. Speed-reading the Scriptures, if they ever begin to concentrate on content, can be a devastating weapon, but happily their pride and our vigilance will see to it that this does not occur.

Beyond this trivial concern, you mentioned something that can be of really significant importance in returning your patient to our camp. I am speaking about your allusion to his having doubts both about his "security" and even his conversion itself. Now here is a real opportunity to fan this small spark into a raging inferno of Satanic psychological warfare. Doubt, as every young fiend ought to know, is father to the full-blown thought of unbelief. By permitting himself to doubt, your patient has really called into question the veracity and dependability of the Enemy's Word.

Quite naturally he does not recognize this at the moment, and hopefully he never will until it is too late. Ever since our Father demonstrated the inferiority of the Enemy's creative ability by planting the seeds of doubt in the lady, Eve, we have found it to be one of our most versatile and successful allies. It is no wonder that the Enemy designates it as a sin, a fact we never tire of minimizing to the human race and maximizing in our advanced courses on temptation and seduction at the College. Christians who would recoil in mortal horror and fear from such overtly blatant sins as murder, adultery, blasphemy, and falsehood often readily embrace doubt, blissfully unaware that this is a prime origin of all the others. At every opportunity your patient must be urged to doubt, which is of course the direct opposite of faith, the chief source of power that fuels the Christian life. Psychologically, the humans are creatures of feelings and emotions. Appealing to these traits, you should subtly draw to his attention that he does not "feel" the same way that he once felt when he had his initial conversion experience. Lead him step by step into the valley of depression; here, as he becomes more and more dependent upon his "feeling," he will be less and less influenced by the Enemy's Word. Never let him catch sight of the mature Christian's experience that knows full well the truth that faith in the Enemy and feeling about oneself have no relationship whatever. Fill him with so many doubts about so many things that he never has time to realize that his redemption rests *not* upon how he feels but on what the Enemy did for him and promises to do in the future.

Your goal must be to make your patient eternally insecure; the more he leans upon his feelings, emotions, and theological speculations, the closer you are to its realization. If the furnace of doubt is consistently fueled by the absence of prayer, resistance to the Enemy's Spirit, and sloppy study of His Word, his faith in the Enemy will be successfully eroded and he will feel himself abandoned. Caution must, however, be your watchword, for the Enemy really does love the vile little worms and has promised that they will never be permitted to be separated from that "love." If you give Him but the slightest opportunity, His agents are ever ready to assure your patient that his love for the Enemy is irrefutable proof that He does indeed care, for it is all too obvious that they love Him because He first loved them! This whole nauseating concept continues to defy the best resources of our research and development facilities below, but I have been assured by Lower Command that a major breakthrough is imminent, and then we will be able to expose for all hades and heaven alike to see what must be the selfish nature of His so-called affection for creation.

Relative to the subject of so-called "eternal security" which you bring up, it is a usable concept because it can cause the patient to become complacent. In fact, some of our greatest successes have been with those who thought themselves so eternally secure that they could sin with impunity. We have an interest in keeping up the controversy between such persons and those who oppose them in the Christian church, for as long as they are bickering about being secure they will lose sight of the fact that it is the Enemy's grace that both saves and guards disciples. Since they are the benefactors and not the source of grace, it is *His will* that they must reckon with, and it is *His Word* (not their emotions or theories) that will ultimately resolve the issue. They have missed the point that the Enemy promises only one kind of life, and He terms this life "eternal." If, as His Training Manual suggests (N.T., Vol. 22, Ch. 5, vv. 11-13), this is a present possession, then even from the warped perspective of human reason their security is assured and the debate is fruitless. From our viewpoint, however, they are all potentially tidy morsels for our ever-increasing hunger. Hell help us if there is ever a shortage of either pharisaical or philosophical theologians! We have had many a tasty dish as the direct result of their arrogant speculations.

Do not then neglect doubt. Rather, it must be cultivated as the fine flower of unholiness that it is.

Your affectionate uncle,
Screwtape

Letter VI

My Dear Wormwood:

There can be no doubt that your patient is in jeopardy in the church he now attends, due to the zeal and determination of his minister. You must lead him into a more liberal theological environment. From what you tell me, his fiancée's church seems just the right place.

It is of small moment to us that her pastor professes Christianity and so-called Christian love, morality, and ethics. He neither believes the Enemy's gospel nor preaches it, so there is little likelihood that we will lose any souls currently under his influence.

Over the years we have persuaded thousands of such hirelings to enter the ministry, and we have installed them in key positions in seminaries, synods, conferences, and congregations, where they have performed invaluable service to our cause. We always see to it that their motives are reasonably "pure," such as "the service of mankind" or "the redemption of society" or the practice of some "golden rule" or other. In reality, they end up doing for their fellow humans no more than a principled agnostic or atheist could accomplish, particularly if such a person were a psychologist or social worker. Most important, they never even know they have neglected the Enemy's prime concern—the personal deliverance of the human soul from the Kingdom below.

From time to time we also "inspire" prominent liberal clergymen to become "avant garde" (a vacuous but useful term!) in their theology and to deny or redefine out of existence virtually everything the Enemy commands. We persuade them that they are being "true to the essence of the gospel" or "relevant to the contemporary needs of modern man"—champions, if you will, of a "faith for today that works." At one time we had three such accomplished agents, two of them bishops (English and American, I believe) and one of them a German missionary doctor, theologian, and musician. The bishops wrought havoc in their flocks by virtue of their position and writings while the missionary sowed confusion because he was the perfect counterfeit. Who, after all, could fault a many-talented man who gave his life to the service of a primitive people, asking nothing? The fact that he hindered spiritually thousands of those he physically treated and prevented them from entering the Enemy's kingdom escaped his admirers, along with his splendid portrayal of the Enemy's Son as a victim of epilepsy and delusions of grandeur. For this alone he deserved to receive Hell's Medal of Honor, which, I assure you, is of much more enduring recognition that the missionary's Nobel prize.

None of the three, I might add, ever believed the Enemy's Word, and all of them subtly subverted His kingdom and violated their oaths of fealty to His person. Of course, we saw to it that they became famous as living proof that the Enemy could be denied by His own alleged ministers and that they in turn could be tolerated by His professing church. That was one of our better efforts, and it is not, I assure you, an isolated case.

You mentioned that this liberal minister is close in his vocabulary to the Enemy's message. This is as it should be; a good counterfeit must resemble as closely as possible the original. The truth of the matter is that the real trick is to sound orthodox while being heretical. This craft has been honed to razor sharpness by some modern theologians, who have sucked out the substance of the Enemy's Word from the vantage point of their impeccable seminary and pulpit positions and have left only an empty shell of meaningless metaphysics. I believe the Enemy Himself has described it as "a famine for the hearing of the Word of God."

Hopefully your patient will be taken in by this semantic double-think, but be careful that the Enemy's Spirit does not arouse his suspicions. Should this occur, convince him that he is being "unloving" and "judging" in his attitude, and that he must be more tolerant of the views of others. If this fails to quiet him down, have his fiancée remind him that the minister has studied more than your patient has and therefore knows more than he does, so he doesn't really have any right to question his authority or interpretations. Don't let him suspect for a second that the issue is really one of truth versus error, not personal interpretation or opinion. He must not see that the Enemy desires him to put to the test all things that purport to originate with Him no matter who says them, and that it is never unloving or judgmental to question what challenges the Enemy's Word. In point of fact, it is rank disobedience for the Enemy's professed followers not to do this.

But if you can obscure these facts, there is a good chance that he will embrace what hell considers to be the perfect synonym for true religion—churchianity. In this marvelous imitation of the Enemy's church everything looks and sounds right and good, but the Enemy's Spirit is conspicuously absent. You must arrange to make him a devout Methodist or Anglican or Baptist or Presbyterian or what have you. But he must come to accept the church as a type of religious social club where people congregate to be helped and to help each other (a splendid half-truth), not to be redeemed and instructed by the Enemy.

I quite understand your concern over your patient's friends who have pointed out to him the dangers of the so-called "social gospel." Don't be overly concerned; we have dealt effectively with this before.

Fortunately, the ever-festering fundamentalist-liberal controversy in the Christian church can be utilized to serve our aims.

Suggest to him that the fundamentalists are perennially unloving and pharisaical about certain doctrinal minutia and are prone to stifling legalisms which really have nothing whatever to do with what the Enemy requires for the life He desires them to live. Be sure to have her minister preach a sermon which underlines the importance of "serving God through serving your fellowman" and use this to accuse the fundamentalists of a lack of concern for minorities, ghettos, and varied other legitimate social concerns with which they have studiously avoided becoming involved. He is not sufficiently advanced to see the fallacy of this reasoning nor enough of a student of the history of the church to realize that its record of social achievement stems directly from the Enemy's commitment to human needs. This commitment He has been quite successful in implementing through remarkably faithful servants who have a disturbing fidelity to orthodox rather than heretical theology. No matter, because the charge that the fundamentalists (or evangelicals, as some of them prefer to be called) have avoided basic issues involving social concern cannot be denied, though over the long run they do have an amazing capacity to care for other humans on the basis of what they disgustingly refer to as "Christian love."

Just be certain that your patient notices only the defects

of fundamentalism and only the virtues of liberalism. In our Father's grand plan the liberals will emphasize social concern at the expense of spiritual regeneration, and the evangelicals regeneration at the expense of social commitment. We must never permit the two to be joined together, as it would undo centuries of careful planning by our Propaganda Division.

By the way, we do have valuable allies in the heart of the Enemy's camp made up of a group who eschew fundamentalism *and* liberalism and are characterized principally by a desire to believe parts of the Enemy's message liberally diluted by destructive criticism of His Training Manual. This permits them to have their spiritual and intellectual cake and eat it, too. Such persons can be of real value to you in presenting your patient with a living contradiction. Here is the spectacle of people who affirm the essence of the Enemy's message while doubting and questioning its absolute inspiration and authority. One of this type has lately become prominent and influential in a high post—the largest society for distributing the Enemy's Word on earth. Exposure to people of this kind will further serve to confuse your patient's judgment concerning his fiancée's minister and will generally cloud the entire atmosphere of his spiritual life with the gnawing doubt that perhaps what he has learned from his own minister is not as "scholarly" or "dependable" as his own newfound interpretations of Christianity. Whatever you do, keep him in a constant environment of change—destroy whatever faith he may have in the permanency of anything, particularly the Enemy's gospel. In a word, help him to become more religious, but for hell's sake and your own, not more Christian!

Your affectionate uncle,
SCREWTAPE

Letter VII

My Dear Wormwood:

It is no use your attempting to explain your failure to keep your patient occupied in his fiancée's church, but how could you ever have run the risk of letting both of them attend an evangelistic crusade? You know full well our Father's feelings where that particular evangelist is concerned. He has quite literally been a thorn in our flesh for almost three decades, and the Enemy's interest in him has been the sole reason why we have not been able to successfully entrap him in the past. I am fully aware that he is both unsophisticated and relatively untrained and that he is forever exhorting the humans to leave their seats and made a decision to serve the Enemy. But one cannot successfully argue with the results he has had, and your conceit in thinking that you could prevent him from exerting an influence over your patient has resulted in your temporary setback. What transpired, of course, is that the Enemy's Spirit, always ready to take an unfair advantage, persuaded your patient that he needed to "rededicate his life" to the Enemy's cause, and this resulted in his returning to his own church where he first began his spiritual pilgrimage. His fiancée, too, felt a need to change her spiritual environment, and I am confident that neither of them realizes just how close they were to spiritual sterilization in her church, though that area of temptation must now be considered a complete loss. While this is tragic from our perspective, there are some lessons to be learned, and everything you did was not a total failure.

Despite the Enemy's apparent victory, you did succeed in getting your patient out of the arena before the Enemy's follow-up team could speak with him or disseminate their damnable packet of unusually effective literature. Since he is essentially an introvert, remind him of how many persons were present, how well-organized the entire operation was, and, of course, how much money was collected. Play on his emotions and his dislike for big choirs and overly friendly people. Whatever you do, don't let him forget the time spent by the evangelist's associates in introducing celebrities and hawking their various books, records, tapes, and "free gifts," all designed to enlarge the evangelist's mailing lists. In the world of daily business your patient would not think of objecting to such practices to increase the distribution of his own products. But cultivate in him a sense of sacrilege that the servants of the Enemy should be just as zealous in the promotion of His product, which, unfortunately, continues to sell rather well despite our redoubled efforts.

We were indeed fortunate that the evangelist unknowingly played right into our hands by having those talented black persons worship the Enemy in a form of music totally abhorrent to your patient. As you have observed, he already has some racist background (newly renounced), and that fact, coupled with the evangelist's topic that evening on "sex and the single person," went a long way toward offending your patient's sense of propriety. It appeared, in his eyes, to cast the evangelist in the role of a meddler, and I think there is a real opportunity here to make some inroads. I am therefore recommending that Lechmore and Snobsnivel, who are experts in sex and racism, respectively, come to your assistance. Unfortunately, Legion is occupied elsewhere for the moment.

So far your patient has abstained from sexual activities he previously enjoyed and has respected the Enemy's advice and admonitions. It has been our experience, however, that the natural sex drive which the Enemy intended for procreation and pleasure can be wonderfully perverted. It can be subtly channeled so that it is eventually exploited purely for sensual pleasure outside the Enemy's prescribed boundaries of matrimony. Your patient is surely aware of the physical attributes of his fiancée and is attracted to her. Thus the inclination toward illicit sex exists. You must now strive to create the environment and the opportunity for its consummation. When you tempt sexually, keep the patient rationalizing in his mind regarding both the motivation and ultimate goal of expressing his sexual feelings. Encourage him to remember that "sex can't be all bad" because, after all, the Enemy made it, and that since he intends to marry the lady, there should really be no guilt attached to it. Bring his attention wherever possible to modern trends which have revolutionized the "puritanical" customs of the past and have banished any real problems of disease or conception through the panacea of modern drugs and the pill.

Convince him that because they really "love" each other, abstinence from premarital sex is an invasion of their basic right to express that "love." Besides, nothing could be really wrong just so long as no one "gets hurt." Conjure up, if possible, the concept of actual psychological and physiological harm if one does not express his or her "God-given drives," and that surely sex is a legitimate member of this family of emotions. All of these tactics, you realize, are constructed so as to obscure the fact that he is really desirous of exploiting his fiancée for his own personal gratification, as well as the equally disturbing truth that the Enemy he is now committed to serve absolutely forbids it. He will never be closer to Eden than when he first begins to rationalize from experience rather than rest upon faith.

See to it, then, that they are alone a great deal of the time, if at all possible, and put him in contact with some of the modern pornography which both the media and magazines systematically encourage. Stimulate him to read some of the more boldly advertised sexually oriented publications on the excuse that the magazines contain "worthwhile contributions" to society and culture. Help him to justify his puerile interest on the ground that the female figure is part of the Enemy's creation and therefore to be admired. One of our most recent triumphs was to have a film made on the life of a famous war hero noted for his blasphemous and obscene statements. We allowed it to attain international prominence on the grounds that it was "depicting life as it really is," thus justifying its vulgarity. Such an approach will doubtless begin to arouse him, so that he tolerates the vulgar and the sexually oriented in whatever place he finds it—a big step toward the ultimate goal of practice on his own part. Along this line of reasoning we have, of late, received some real support from the clergy.

One of our clerical allies has, in fact, virtually justified all forms of sexual aberration by insisting upon the "new concept" that personal human ethics must be based upon each individual situation one encounters. This was a magnificent accomplishment on the part of Lechmore and Tallbrow, who led the learned professor and theologian into the oldest ethical error of all—the practice of evil in the pursuit of goodness. In the Enemy's name he has convinced millions of humans that their moral and sexual behavior is to be governed not by the lofty pronouncements of the Enemy's Training Manual but by the particular situation in which they find themselves! Your patient should become acquainted with his writings as rapidly as possible, as these will serve to further erode his respect for the Enemy's Word and Christian ethical judgments. Be sure in all this, Wormwood, that he never sees that the Enemy has provided a way out of his dilemma. He has promised that He will not permit your patient to be tempted beyond his powers of resistance and, in fact, guarantees a way of escape from us to all who trust Him. Your patient must not guess this, but instead must come to accept our influence as an all-powerful and never-diminishing presence. This is, of course, quite untrue, because the Enemy has historically restricted our best efforts with His usual meddling and interfering tactics.

All in all, however, the more we secularize your patient or make him worldly, the more we can convince him that moral and ethical judgments are relative to the culture and the situation rather than to the absolute standard of the Enemy's will. From that point on we can lead him to explore the sexual delicatessen that our studied efforts have made of human morality. Hell's best interests are never better served than by encouraging our patients to pursue evil under the guise of good. The "way that seems right" thus becomes under our molding techniques the broad road to eternal spiritual death. Therefore promote their "secular cities," exalt their "new morality," promulgate their sexual explorations, and stimulate their "situation ethics," for in the end we shall make what the Enemy intended for good to become an ultimate exercise in triumphant evil.

Your affectionate uncle,
SCREWTAPE

Letter VIII

My Dear Wormwood:

What a pleasant surprise to learn from your last letter that you have driven a wedge of disagreement between your patient and his new wife. This is a devilishly bad move and will have the effect, if sustained, of pushing them hellward while they are literally pulling each other apart.

Personally speaking, she exerts too good an influence over him and is rather stubbornly resistant to our advances now that she has gotten into one of those accursed women's groups that systematically studies the Enemy's Manual and harps on prayer and praise to Him.

Don't pass up the opportunity of suggesting to him that she ought to spend more time at home meeting his needs rather than traipsing off to Christian hen parties. Actually, we know she is very faithful to her wifely obligations, but he must be led to think otherwise. Her religious activities must be made to appear as an encroachment upon his time, which affords us real opportunities for precipitating arguments.

Now of course you realize that she is perfectly correct in asserting the fact that she is entitled to be more than a shadow or reflection of her husband, and further that the Enemy does not expect her to be his alter ego. It is obvious that as a woman she fulfills a singular role as wife and mother, being largely occupied with the home as both its chief stabilizing factor and the moving force that influences the children. Occupying this important role, therefore, she is a target we cannot afford to pass up. Here in hell at the regular sessions of the Lucifer Club, veteran tempters often regale younger fiends with case history after case history of how strong husbands (and especially clergymen) have been successfully neutralized and disrupted through their wives after having resisted our efforts everywhere else. They just never expected us to attack the so-called "weaker vessel."

They know better now! Encourage her, then, to be submissive to her husband, but only to the point where she agrees with his judgment — when that happens, substitute "servitude" for submission in her thinking and "assertion of her personhood" for what is really rebellion against his authority. This type of conflict, if nurtured and if children are involved (particularly after a few years of marriage), has served our ends in multiple instances and has resulted in myriads of broken homes and tortured souls. Hell preserve us if they ever learn that no wife will ever find it difficult to love and obey her husband if she knows that he loves her as much as he loves himself! But this is another subject.

I recall one case in particular where we used the technique of marital tension to produce utterly hellish results.

The lady in question after some fifteen years of matrimony had fallen victim to a philosophy that today permeates many affluent societies. We have come to term it in our training sessions "the self-pity plague." At any rate, the lady in this case succumbed to the belief that life was passing her by and that her husband and children did not appreciate her sacrifices and accomplishments. We immediately planted the seed that she was "taken for granted" and was "everybody's slave." After consulting with other dissatisfied and disillusioned "homemakers" in a similar mind set, she became more convinced than ever that she was living in a creative vacuum, on a treadmill of boredom, and was on her way to middle-aged oblivion.

When a vocal feminist and women's liberationist exhorted the local female population to "discover your destiny" and "find your real self," she knew that her deliverance was at hand and openly applauded her emancipation. I well recall how hard we worked at conditioning her for this great moment by encouraging her to believe she possessed talents, resources, and gifts that were in reality only figments of her imagination and our suggestions. How hard we labored to convince her that inside all people are boundless abilities which only lack the opportunity and will to act, and that at heart everyone is a frustrated author, statesman, doctor, lawyer, actor, artist, or whatever else such "self-expressive" thinking desires! What she did not realize and most humans still do not realize, of course, is that man is limited and his talents generally mediocre at best.

But we continued to sustain the illusion for her, and by appealing to her pride and "dignity as a liberated woman," we literally shamed her into feeling that only her version of "creative self-expression" could justify her femininity and marriage. Her already-liberated colleagues disparaged her role of wife and mother and extolled the virtues of the liberated life, until gradually she became incapable of separating reality from delusion. Think of it! She was *only* a wife and mother (formerly status symbols among the humans), but now she had become a "creative person." Of course this is all rubbish, as if one could not be a creative person in being a wife and mother! But she was so intent on "self-expression" that she never realized this until it was too late for anything but tears.

Our supreme triumph came in her case when we "illumined" her about her religion. We persuaded her that the Enemy's church was just another form of male chauvinism, a priestly oppression and exploitation of womanhood that the emanicipated woman didn't need, since it demanded submission now for benefits to be bestowed hereafter. The "bird in the hand is worth two in the bush" maxim worked perfectly, and she literally threw the baby out with the bathwater and abandoned church altogether. We, in effect, got her (as we must get your patient's wife) to lose sight of the fact that the Enemy never promised perfection on earth nor, for that matter, constant happiness, creativity, or total self-expression for all men.

Rather, the Enemy promised peace of soul and mind by making peace with Him. Of course, this is just another of His spiritual carrots perpetually dangled before the human donkeys as a tantalizing reward that they will never obtain. We shall see to that, you may be sure; in fact, we have already convinced many of the humans that all the Enemy really offers is relief in the next life from the cruelties and injustices in this one. They must not discover that He does grant an amazing amount of gratification, satisfaction, joy, and so-called blessings to those who obey His will. This is all, of course, rather sophomoric behavior for someone who is supposed to know everything and whose will is allegedly irresistible. But be on guard anyway against any of this penetrating the mind of your patients. In the case that I have outlined, our persistence won out!

It all worked wonderfully well for us on the whole, but thank hell she never suspected and examined our tactics. Today she is divorced, has given up her children, is both a work and college dropout, and wallows in a semialcoholic sea of self-pity, welfare checks, and unsatisfying sexual liaisons. She is bitter at the Enemy (a superb by-product of our efforts), bored with her emancipation, frightened, and tormented. Her children no doubt understand that she is the victim of exploitation on everyone's part and that the male-dominated power structure in society, not she, is to blame for the consequences of her actions. To this day she is largely unaware that for the flimsiest reasons she left a husband and children who loved her, a good home, the respect of her community, and the fellowship of her church—largely because fulfilling the role of wife and mother was exchanged for the overworked but still valuable illusion that the grass is always greener in the next yard.

Fortunately for our cause, this plague so graphically outlined for you is virulently contagious. So you see, Wormwood, no opportunity to capitalize upon human weakness and sow chaos in the Enemy's established order of society must be overlooked. Your patient's wife is particularly vulnerable in these areas due to her previous social influences and her strong will. Study what I have set forth and see if with a little innovation here and there you cannot duplicate my results in your patient's marriage. Remember always our Father's marriage motto for the humans— "What heaven joins together, hell puts asunder."

Your affectionate uncle,
SCREWTAPE

Letter IX

My Dear Wormwood:

You are making splendid progress with your patient, and I am delighted that he is now obsessed with solving the paradox of faith and works which the Enemy permits to exist in His so-called "divine plan." Allow him a wide latitude to explore the nature of his "faith" in the Enemy. This is an infantile exercise in pure gullibility at best, since as of the moment he is not really capable of defining it to himself, much less explaining it to others! This heavenly poppycock about it being the substance of what is hoped for and the evidence of the intangible has apparently escaped him for the moment, but guard against his rediscovering it, lest you jeopardize your own position. At the moment he thinks that the word "faith" always means the same thing (a real triumph for Triptweeze and the Language Department below), though this is, of course, a grand delusion. For review purposes, remember that there are various types of faith and that we can make good use of all of them.

The first in the category is present in all the humans

whenever they are threatened by immediate danger or death. Its basic root is fear, not love of the Enemy. During wartime combat, for instance, the soldier under fire "believes" that the Enemy can preserve him from injury and death because in his soul he remembers his Creator. But when the crisis of the moment is past he returns to his former ways immediately, having never truly repented of anything—still unregenerate and still ours for the taking! They never seem to learn that the Enemy only delivers those who recognize that they are lost and commit themselves without doubt to His charge. It is all totally unrealistic and vaguely reminiscent of the cock-and-bull story the Enemy gave our Father below shortly before his rapid exit from the realms above.

A second variety, to which your patient has already been exposed as a child, is what is known as inculcated faith. The victim of this perversion of hell learns his or her religion much as they learn reading and writing—that is, by constant repetition of creedal propositions. The profanation of the sacred is thus accomplished by subtly substituting memory for experience and shadow for substance. It is very similar to singing a nursery rhyme in a foreign language; the pronunciation and accent may be memorized perfectly, but without translation it is utterly meaningless. Let him learn the doctrine of the Enemy in this fashion, but just be certain he does not stumble across the translation!

Objective faith is still another type we consistently use with growing success in an age where scientism and inductive thought are deemed to be the only access to reality and truth. In this framework we need not resist his objective analysis of the material contained in the Enemy's Training Manual as long as we are able to separate the facts from personal experience. For example, there are untold numbers of people who "believe" in the Enemy's existence, His concern for mankind, and even the distorted trivia of His so-called redemptive plan for all creation. They may even give assent to that notorious event at Bethlehem some millennia ago, the unfortunate incident about a cross (which our Father so rightly questions), and even that second encounter in a garden which cost our Father his dominion over death.° All of these things are accepted by such persons much as one accepts the historicity of King George III or General Washington. They have missed the point that, though they may study all about such characters and become intimate with many events of their lives, they have never known those individuals personally, having mistaken knowledge *about* them for experience *with* them— an error we must continue to cultivate and nurture. Knowing all about the Enemy, therefore, is not to be confused with knowing Him on a personal level, and today there are countless souls in our Father's house below who failed to make this differentiation.

Then, as you will doubtless recall, there is a final kind of bogus faith which feeds hell on a large scale and is properly designated subjective. This category is occupied by individuals who revolt against all objective criteria and base everything upon their feelings or emotions. They have a "feeling" about their relationship to the Enemy which does not bear the slightest resemblance to what He really requires, but this does not appear to disturb them. They seldom study His Training Manual, and even if they manage to do so, it is always seen through the jaundiced eyes of their depraved emotions. The Enemy, they assert, is a God of love, and because their feelings prohibit it there cannot possibly be a hell to which His justice would consign them or, for that matter, anyone else. They "feel" that there must be many paths to the kingdom above, so that, contrary to His assertion that the gate is narrow, they never tire of widening it to admit almost anyone. Oblivious to the Enemy's warnings and blissful in sharing the abundance of

---

° *A possible reference to Matthew chapter 28 and the Resurrection.*

their own ignorance, they follow their "inner convictions" and shape the image of the Enemy in their manifestly deficient likeness. We have promoted their generous feelings toward each other but have kept the basis of such generosity veiled from their spiritual eyes. The truth is that sinners can well afford to be generous with each other—they are all under the same condemnation! It is only when they see themselves not in the light of individual comparison but in comparison with *Him* that they can at last perceive how perilously close they are to joining us here at our Father's throne. But for some perverse reason the kind of faith the Enemy requires is by its very nature disquieting because it is transforming. Nothing is quite so disruptive to our best efforts than a veteran sinner who becomes a new type of creature and who considers himself to be the Enemy's temple. The life that is changed and which reflects the energizing presence and power of the Enemy's Spirit is productive of fruit and becomes a recipient of spiritual gifts that enable the individual to become a zealous and even conquering disciple. Should your patient start to engage in such activities, introduce him to the paradox of faith versus works.

Direct his attention to passages in the Enemy's Training Manual which talk of his having been acquitted before the bar of the Enemy's "justice" on the basis of *both* faith and works, thus conveniently diverting his attention from the true basis of his redemption, which the Enemy naively calls "grace." Prevent him at all costs from discovering that there are in reality two types of justification in which the Enemy is interested. It is obvious that only the Enemy can see genuine faith, and that on this basis He exonerates His followers from the penalty of their sin. Equally obvious is the fact that *men* can know of the reality of faith only when they observe works which testify to its existence. Such works the Enemy demands as *proof of* and not the *means of* individual "salvation," as He terms it. Acquittal by both

faith and by works is undoubtedly the Enemy's scheme—
the one kind of acquittal before His throne and the other
kind before man and the universe. However, as long as we
can confuse the two and stop your patient from learning
that the Enemy's grace is the root of the whole thing, he
may well become bogged down in one of the other types of
faith I have described, and then, by hell, we have him!

Your affectionate uncle,
SCREWTAPE

Letter X

My Dear Wormwood:

I have been giving a great deal of consideration to the question that you raised in your last report. Incidentally, I hope that you keep all of our correspondence on a confidential level, particularly any references I may have made to Dragonslik or Slubgob. You realize, of course, that I was simply jesting when I made allusions to certain areas of weakness in the Intelligence Division and ineptitude at the Training College. Occasionally we all make uncomplimentary remarks, but rest assured it is of a constructively critical nature and should not be passed on lest regrettable misunderstandings arise. You know I will always look out for your interests and, as you know, have shielded you on occasion from the pryings of certain higher authorities who have evidenced some degree of hostility toward you, particularly in regard to certain inconsistencies in your reports. Naturally I know you will reciprocate, and I'm sure you are aware that I have only the highest regard and respect for both Dragonslik and Slubgob.

Now to the matter at hand. I think it is safe for you to proceed on the assumption that your patient's quick temper or "low boiling point," as he often terms it, can bear real fruit in disrupting his relationships with his fellow Christians and in his home and office life as well. Over the centuries we have observed that anger has been one of our most successful methods of alienating members of the human family from each other. In fact, it ranks with hate (which incidentally it produces), anxiety, impatience, gluttony, and lust as useful tools found not only in the armory of hell but in what the Enemy terms the carnal or rebellious nature of man. Even the Enemy has observed that anger is an "outrage" and that "wrath is cruel." He goes so far as to designate it one of the "works of the flesh," that which produces unrighteousness (you are well aware that He classifies all unrighteousness as "sin"). He has commanded that all those who would walk with Him must cease from anger, and He terms those who abstain from it as "wise."

As usual, He is guilty of oversimplification, because any fool knows that if He is the supreme example, as He maintains, He should be the last one to be angry at our Father, and yet His own Training Manual is studded with illustrations of His own anger! Of course, it could be argued that there is such a thing as righteous anger, but, as one of earth's most celebrated writers once put it, "nothing is either good or bad, but thinking makes it so." That is, by the way, is a very fine illustration of how to sound profound while practicing self-deception. It is obvious that things are good in themselves or bad in themselves depending on whether they find their source of authority in our concepts or in those of the Enemy. Those foolish enough to think that the Enemy is right label everything which opposes His standards as "wrong," whereas those who are in agreement with us (either by overt affirmation or unwillingness to endorse the Enemy's position) declare for our position. Only the terribly naive or uninformed think good and evil are relative to human experience or philosophy. We labor, of course, to obscure this tactic from the humans, but occasionally one of them does see through it.

But pure anger can definitely be a violently disruptive force in the Christian life of your patient, for only anger can fragment longstanding friendships and can turn brother against brother, husband against wife, family against family, and, inevitably in its most exquisite form, nation against nation. It was the senseless anger of Agamemnon that gave us the Trojan wars and the destruction of Troy. Contrary to popular historical novels and romantic rubbish, it was not the face of Helen that launched a thousand ships but the anger of her cuckolded husband! A word spoken in anger can never be retracted or obliterated from the memory of the offended person. Let me be quick to suggest that in your patient's case it is imperative that he find some reason to justify his anger so that his Christian conscience will not be totally offended. He will be casting about for various means of rationalizing his conduct, so be certain to bring to his attention that whether it be employee, relative, or spouse, they were in some measure responsible for his explosive outburst. Do not let him see that the real responsibility rests with him, since if he were really trusting in what the Enemy irritatingly refers to as His grace, your patient would have found his angry outburst unnecessary.

In the matter of domestic problems which can be aggravated by anger, do all within your power to prolong his angry attitude, making sure that he does not resolve it before he goes to bed. Since your patient is a being of spirit as well as of physical form, his spirit may be communicated with while he is asleep as well as when he is awake. Nothing does more to prolong the long-range effects of anger than sleeping on it. The Enemy has anticipated this, and your patient must not discover that while anger in itself is sin, "letting the sun go down" upon anger magnifies and enhances its effect. Alas, the number of marriages which have been able to withstand our best efforts because the husband and wife have agreed to settle their differences before the day is over, usually resolving them in emotional reconciliation and with the Enemy's help in prayer! Be sure to encourage your patient to have his "family devotions" with his wife just before bedtime, because if a problem of anger is involved, he will use it as an excuse not to "have devotions," thus discouraging communication with his wife and with the Enemy. On the other hand, when anger is absent, encourage him to have devotions at such a late hour of the day, after the rigors of his job and the normal tensions of matrimony have taken their toll, that he will be exhausted and generally unreceptive and will literally fall asleep while communicating with the Enemy. To watch your patient trail off his prayers with a snore is a sweet taste of victory indeed and, whether he recognizes it or not, a direct insult to the Enemy.

Along this line, anger works best for us when the object of anger is not aware of it. This permits the angry person to display hostility and frustrate the individual who is exposed to it. It is not necessary to go into detail. The evidence is overwhelming that anger produces in humans every condition ranging from heart attacks and strokes to emotional breakdowns, mental illness, and ulcers. This becomes even more apparent when anger is suppressed, leading to the fallacy that it is a good thing under all circumstances to vent one's anger upon its imagined cause. Such grievous words uttered wrathfully only succeed in stirring up more anger, thereby complicating rather than alleviating the situation. If at all possible, have your patient "confront" those with whom he is angry, for under that mistaken impression there is simply no end to the amount of mischief that can be generated at home, at work, and especially in church.

As I pointed out before, there is a fine line between anger itself for the sake of anger and what the Enemy's

Training Manual refers to as righteous indignation or wrath. There are some things which ought to make us angry and upon which we should express ourselves in no uncertain terms. The Enemy has done this on a number of notable occasions, one of which involved whipping some of our foremost representatives, overturning their tables, and driving them with their merchandise out of His House. Convince your patient to conclude from this example that all anger is the same (one of our most successful fictions) and that even anger at his minister (when he touches upon sensitive areas of your patient's life in his Sunday sermons) is justified on the basis that he is meddling. What the obtuse creatures never seem to learn is that anger is the very root of bitterness, which springs up to defile human relationships and set Christian brother against Christian brother in the context of the church. One instance of recent memory involved a noted Christian leader who felt he had been wronged by some of his "brothers" and therefore harbored feelings of resentment and anger, which, by the time we finished with it, had grown from a smoldering hostility to a full-blown rage. He was so bitter at what he considered a grievous wrong that spiritual defilement and alienation had set in and the stage was set for some public name-calling and damage to the whole cause of the Enemy.

There is nothing we delight to see more than some of the dirty linen of the Enemy's church washed in the laundromat of scandal! Unfortunately for our designs, the Enemy's Spirit spoke to the hearts of His allegedly guilty brothers and they obeyed the Enemy's advice and sought Him out. In the meantime, the Enemy's Spirit had also (to our great annoyance) directed him to portions of the Enemy's Training Manual which unmasked our tactics, so that upon seeing one of his offended brothers he humbly and swiftly confessed his "sin." The root of bitterness was excised, and all our splendid efforts came to naught. They are now busy once again in the Enemy's vineyard, though hopefully some of the scars of the conflict will remain for us to exploit at a later date. In my reference to anger in the church, it should not be overlooked. Frequently in the ministries of faithful servants of the Enemy, they are mightily used by His Spirit to convince men of their need of repentance, and we have found that an excellent way to disrupt this is to cause the individual in need of such spiritual therapy to think that the minister is judging or is directing his sermon principally at him. He flatters himself that the clergyman has singled him out for his private wrath. If he only knew that it was the Enemy's Spirit speaking to all men in such a condition, then we would have no basis on which to stimulate his antagonism! Anger of this type inevitably results in the phenomenon of having "roast preacher" for Sunday dinner and of giving inordinate attention to the failings of the preacher and his family as a means of self-justification for his own conduct. This kind of anger produces strife and generates useful conflicts on all levels in the church. Next to the anger of committees vying for attention from either the pastor or the congregation, this is a top-level form of the exploitation of anger. Concerning your patient's problem, do not let him learn that his low boiling point can be raised an almost infinite number of degrees by remembering the Enemy's counsel and the very practical fact that his anger is his own worst enemy, since he is both physically and mentally worse off by either retaining his anger or venting it in the ways which we have discussed.

One Christian theologian who sensed the need to vent his anger chose a constructive rather than a destructive methodology (the direct opposite of our intentions) and quite regularly chopped many cords of firewood as a natural release for his anger, coupled with prayer to the Enemy and meditation upon His Word. His lifespan has unfortunately been lengthened quite measurably by this procedure. He has both disciplined his tongue and improved or maintained excellent relations with a large segment of his "church family," not to mention the virtually inexhaustible supply of firewood he has been accumulating over the last thirty years!

Since your patient is in the publishing business, he may find out that venting his anger in letters that he never mails, but instead reviews from time to time as a means of demonstrating the wisdom of his restraint of anger, may complicate your activities. So if he should decide to "boil over" in a letter, promote the concept in his mind that he is "righteously indignant" and that "truth is on his side." All in all, anger taken as a whole advances the cause of our Father's kingdom. Only a fool, as the Enemy has pointed out, displays anger openly. Occasionally even the Enemy (purely on the basis of statistical probability) arrives at some pragmatic and dynamic truths. This happens to be one of them.

> Your affectionate uncle,
> SCREWTAPE

Letter XI

My Dear Wormwood:

You have finally done it—you have permitted your patient to inhale the breath, the air of heaven, and to come in contact with the stifling presence of the Enemy's Spirit. It was a disaster that your patient underwent a spiritual re-birth and that this loathesome specimen should receive authority to be called a "son" of the Enemy. But *now* he has gained access to a fearful weapon, the Enemy's promise of awesome power. That power, Wormwood, was first unleashed upon us at Jerusalem in tongues of noxious flame that even now sears to the depths of Satanic memory.

Taking unfair advantage of our Father's momentary surprise, the Enemy poured out His Spirit and, I confess, even the most seasoned tempter recoiled from it. However, we quickly countered His thrust and set about neutralizing its effect.

I suggest that you consider very carefully our past successful methodology if you hope to escape the usual punishment and recoup your position.

Your patient has, from our perspective, become the recipient of what the Enemy's Training Manual describes as "the promise of the Father." Some of the Enemy's ser-vants describe the phenomenon as "a filling," "a baptism," or "an enduement of power." Still others (lucky for us) deny or ignore it entirely. But for our purposes it is an influx of enormous energy that manifests itself in various "gifts" for the (obviously selfish) glorification of the Enemy and the strengthening of His forces.

Under the influence of this alien Spirit, the humans display vast quantities of faith, wisdom, and knowledge. They have been known to prophesy, perform miracles, heal the sick, speak in languages unknown to them, interpret the languages, and even judge us! Now all this might appear quite formidable to you at first glance, but we have yet to act!

There are a number of ways we can blunt even this diverse power, so pay close attention. Insofar as we can discern, the quickest and best way to dampen the fervor of those souls newly touched by the Spirit of the Enemy is to mislead them through ignorance and misguide them through pride.

Your patient must be made to feel that his initial emotional experience will continue at the same level of intensity indefinitely and that other Christians that have not shared his experience are somehow less spiritual than he. The former is ignorance, the latter, pride. The Enemy has unwittingly assisted us at this juncture by insisting that His servants be in a constant attitude of receptivity to the Spirit. Since they are in constant need of refilling by Him, they are therefore at His mercy. Because of this they are inevitably forced to come down from their "mountain peak" of ecstasy and enter the valley of trial. At all costs, keep him oriented about his feelings; never let him suspect that what he experienced was based upon the Enemy's Word, not upon his own emotions. If he once succeeds in trusting the Enemy rather than his own feelings, you are in grave danger of failure.

Should this occur, concentrate immediately upon the nature of pride. The patient should be made to feel that his experience is greater than the experience of other Christians. This in turn must be equated in his mind with spiritual superiority, thus in effect reducing his fellow Christians to a second-class citizenship in the Enemy's kingdom. Such an attitude can work wonders of dissension in congregations, and you should be prepared to take advantage of such situations whenever they occur.

There can be no doubt about the fact that the purpose of the Enemy's bestowal of spiritual gifts is to strengthen and build up the church. It therefore becomes fundamental to the realization of our goals that your patient become absorbed with the exercise of whatever gifts he has received, to the exclusion of their main purpose, which is his spiritual maturation as a Christian. The Enemy wishes to build up and strengthen the faith of his organization through the exercise of these gifts, but this can be thwarted if they magnify any one gift to the place where it becomes an obsession and a spiritual status symbol. Encourage such attitudes in your patient wherever feasible because, in the final analysis, it is an overdisplay of lovelessness, the direct opposite of what the Enemy instructed His disciples to have for each other. Abuse of what the Enemy calls His "gifts of grace" is also an excellent way to discourage other Christians from pursuing their possession. If your patient is undisciplined in the exercise of his gifts, then it is possible to use his excesses to force the Enemy to discipline him, or, next best, to cause other Christians to reject totally the Enemy's gifts, thus throwing out the baby with the bathwater.

Last but not least, Wormwood, the indifference and prejudice of many uninformed Christians will aid you many times in successfully resisting the Enemy's inroads into your patient's life.

There are not a few Christians who are indifferent and resistant to any attempt by the Enemy's Spirit to introduce what they term "revival" into their congregations. Some have developed such well-constructed theories of theology and systems of thought that they have not hesitated to limit the Enemy to only one era in which He can bestow His gifts. To hear them tell it, the Enemy is not doing today what He did in the first century of this era, a serious miscalculation by the standards of either hell or heaven! Now as you yourself pointed out, the limiting of the Enemy by any system of interpretation is patently fallacious, but it serves our purposes to assist them in promulgating their theories. We in hell well know the power of the Enemy's Spirit, and our Propaganda Department has designed some marvelous counterfeits of all the Enemy's gifts, a pointless pursuit if the Enemy has withdrawn them. Apparently the humans have not yet learned that hell only counterfeits what heaven creates.

Let me urge you to remember that fear of manifestations from the Enemy's Spirit is widespread in some quarters of His own church. Some even suggest that we are the source of His benevolence. While we cannot deny imitating His power, their own Training Manual points out our limitation, for we cannot answer prayers directed to the Enemy, though we can hinder them.

Do what you can to acquaint your patient with the hostility of some of his fellow Christians toward the new experience he has had. Make sure he sees the abuses that exist within the so-called charismatic movement, and above everything else discourage him from testing all experience by the Enemy's Word, and you will have gone a long way toward robbing him of the joy of his salvation.

The real danger of the Enemy's gifts, as He calls them, is that they will promote what He terms love among His servants and a fervor for spreading His message which we have as yet been unable to prevent or control successfully. Keep up the bad work.

Your affectionate uncle,
SCREWTAPE

Letter XII

My Dear Wormwood:

From your last letter I gather that your patient has been caught up in controversy about what has become known as "the war in Indochina" or "the war in Palestine." This can be a superb opportunity to focus his mind upon the temporal at the not-so-obvious expense of the eternal.

As we remarked once before (and you should have learned this by now!) the Enemy has made humans citizens of time and potentially of eternity. But overemphasis upon either one of these upsets His prescribed balance and creates openings for us. By concentrating your patient's interest exclusively upon his supposed heavenly future, it is possible to make his life of little earthly value in the present. Conversely, by occupying his time solely with the conditions of the present, we can all but eliminate any serious reflection about his eternal future.

Both emphases work well, depending on the climate of the times and your patient's circumstances. I recall, in one of our earlier and more successful campaigns, that we persuaded a large segment of the Enemy's followers to expect the so-called "rapture" (a figment of the Enemy's propaganda) by the year 1000, a good round figure for promotional purposes! Of course it did not occur, but the accompanying disillusionment was so disruptive, and so many came over to our Father's side as a result of the mockery and embarrassment we generated in the world, that we are making plans to repeat the effort again.

Our new approach will center on the myth of the rapture occurring by the year 2000. By a careful manipulation of prophetic speculation, current events, and human imagination, we hope to prepare the Enemy's gullible followers in this age for even greater disappointments to come. A by-product of all this is to occupy their minds with the future while the Enemy's prime directive of carrying his message *to*, while meeting the needs *of*, a desperate humanity is allowed to atrophy. This is the genius of His Satanic Sinfulness, who has termed it the "evil Samaritan syndrome." Never let them think of the hungry, the homeless, and the deprived or how to minister to them. Keep them so heavenly-minded that they are of no earthly good. Of course there are those in the Enemy's camp who do make quite a plausible case (based upon the prejudiced record of the Enemy's Training Manual) for the ultimate return of that One whose name our Father has forbidden us to mention. In fact, they even emphasize concern and care for their fellow humans. But we have historically managed to have the fanatic gain the attention of his brothers and drown the others in a sea of irrelevant prophetic charts, films, and conferences which we encourage as mutual admiration societies. No one ever really applies any of these things practically. They just articulate them as a convenient means of salving their consciences without obeying the Enemy's Word.

So never pass up this kind of opportunity. It has many fringe benefits. By the way, Wormwood, don't neglect the other side of the coin, so to speak. There are those in the Enemy's camp who direct so much attention to the social, economic, and political redemption of men in the Enemy's name that they minimize the spiritual dimension of the humans and substitute social for spiritual salvation (forgive the word!). They are first-rate allies for our cause if we are careful in handling them. The so-called "do-gooder" is really transformed under our tutelage to an "evildoer" because he can be taught to make human works an attempted means of justifying his life and thereby "saving" his soul, a practice the Enemy resolutely rejects. We must keep the humans from seeing that, contrary to what they think, human nature is essentially corrupt at its core, thanks to our Father's glorious victory over the first humans in Eden. There at the outset he defeated the Enemy and staked hell's claim to the whole race. We do not object to their "good works," then, as long as we can attribute them to "humanity" and not to the so-called "providence" of the Enemy, who, it is mistakenly believed, causes it to rain on the just and the unjust. Our task is to get them so entangled in the affairs of earth that heaven is just a dim afterthought in the gray haze of the future. Keep the future hazy and keep the present confused, occupied, and consistently noisy. No man can be a good soldier if he is so occupied, and we must encourage, along with fuzzy-minded ideas, such fruitless pursuits.

However, these things aside, the Vietnam War, as the Americans prefer to call it, has certain real possibilities. In speaking with Rabbleprod, who is in direct demonic charge of all successful mob activities, and Swinesnoop, the head of all police and governmental intelligence agencies on earth, I have learned that college riots, protest marches, free-speech rallies, etc. can serve our purposes if properly exploited. Since your patient is disposed toward pacifism and nonviolence, involve him in such things wherever possible. It is amazing how many normally nonviolent, peaceful, liberty-loving persons can be transformed by mob emotions and "a just cause" into violent, aggressive, demagogic tyrants. You are perfectly right in noting that they seem to make a religion of their patriotism or lack of it and that they break the law or use it to suit their need. This can, of course, profit us greatly.

We count as one of our greatest triumphs the fact that frequently those who cry the loudest for free speech have been incited by Rabbleprod's cunning and Swinesnoop's provocation to forbid others what, paradoxically, they demand for themselves, namely, the right to speak. Watching them shout down the "loyal opposition" and abuse with obscenities those whose only crime is disagreeing with their point of view is a triumph of Satanic tactics indeed. The patient need not go to such extremes, but if we can make him intolerant of the views of others, persuade him that lawlessness is justified for good causes (namely those he's interested in), and use a "cause" as a lever to pry him away from his religious commitment, then we will have struck the Enemy a severe blow.

Your patient must not be permitted to analyze his reasons for so acting—substitute reaction for thinking. People must be conditioned to react to all different types of situations. They must not be permitted to think. The image in his mind of a war-ravaged land, starving children, and senseless brutality must be connected to political intrigue and to unscrupulous leaders of "power structures" who manipulate the public and manage the news media. Incidentally, we have found the term "power structure" most applicable as a catchall target for everyone's anger. For the minorities it is white, and for the majority it is black. In the case of the student and the amateur analyst, it is the Pentagon or the CIA, whereas the liberal and the conservative describe it as right-wing and left-wing respectively. Capitalism fixes the blame on Communism, and Communism accuses democracy. The rich point to the discontented poor and the poor to the greed of the wealthy.

As long as we can keep them from learning the truth—that all of them share in the guilt of a world ruled not by them but by our Father, and that at the root of their problem is their sin and our demonic exploitation of it—we shall continue to divide and conquer. It is obvious that your patient is ripe for the espousal of a cause; very well, then, give him one and let him pursue it to the exclusion of all his other activities. Convince him that he is sacrificing time for "the good of humanity" (a fine cliche we coined!). Get him to work for it and believe in it absolutely.

We have found that devotion to political personages works quite acceptably here. One of the Enemy's former servants succumbed to this approach in a recent election campaign and worked so hard for his "idol" (I do not jest) that one would have thought that the candidate was running for Messiah instead of President! He soon lost all interest in his church, home, family, friends, and business. He sacrificed, in his own mind, everything for "the cause." He ended up thinking only of the cause. When his idol was smashed in the great iconoclastic controversy of the electorate, he suffered a heart seizure and is now safe below in our Father's house. Diligence is what made the difference, and we must remain so if we are going to prove the Enemy's Training Manual false and enthrone our Father as the true Lord of Light. Admittedly, we do have some serious obstacles here. But things are looking darker day by day and, happily, blacker by the century.

Your affectionate uncle,
SCREWTAPE

Letter XIII

My Dear Wormwood:

You surprise me by your all-too-evident poor grounding in the subject of misdirection, particularly where your patient's business life is involved.

The business he is engaged in (I believe publishing) has been a fertile field for us almost from its start, and you have a real opportunity to continue our progress in your patient's firm. As an aside and on the matter of misdirection in the area of your own activities relative to our correspondence (which I instructed you to keep confidential), you will no doubt be surprised to learn that I have explained all the confidential matters you raised to the complete satisfaction of Swinesnoop and the SSP.° He fully understands that you were attempting to attribute to my counsel some of your own ridiculous blunders. As I suggested in earlier correspondence, I urge you to peruse the revised and profusely illustrated booklet issued by The House of Correction for

---

° *Satanic Secret Police*

Incompetent Tempters. You will find it extremely instructive, particularly those pages dealing with punishments for disloyalty *to* and slander *against* one's superiors.

The subject of your patient's business activities must not be obscured by this personal matter between us, which I assure you will be resolved. The task at hand is to use business opportunities to both discredit his Christian walk and (since his is a large publishing house) effectively misrepresent or dilute what the Enemy desires to disseminate.

As you suggested, our opportunities multiply now that he has left his secular publishing job and joined a Christian publishing firm. He is still suffering, no doubt, from the concept that the secular world and the religious world are essentially different in their business ethics and basic goals, so it will come as a shock to him to find out that many times the ethics of non-Christians and their principles of morality are superior to those of professing believers. He has felt that leaving the "worldly" publishing field and entering that devoted to the proclamation of the Enemy's position will permit him the opportunity for Christian fellowship and a striving for goals that could not be recognized in the secular arena. Let him go on thinking that, and be certain to direct him to those members of his new employer's firm that are worldly Christians devoted to the pursuit of pleasure, money, and security and who place their religion secondary to their greed and ambition. Persons such as this make a great deal about the subject of Christian liberty when in reality they are only seeking license to live as they previously lived prior to their conversion. They look down upon those they term "weaker brothers" in the faith and count their excesses as evidence of maturity or superiority. Yes, by all means, put him and keep him in contact with such persons.

Christian publishers exert enormous influence over the Christian public and, to be sure, most of them discharge their responsibilities in a fashion most irritating to our aims. But we have found over the years that, like all humans, they are vulnerable to greed and what has been termed the "sweet smell of success." His immediate superior is one such person, a man who maintains the facade and vocabulary of the Christian faith but has long ago had his conscience seared with the hot iron of worldly ambition and avarice. He maintains his position because he is valuable to the firm on the level of accomplishment, but they are largely unaware of his shoddy and questionable practices.

He has even influenced those who formulate policy in the publishing house to the place where he exercises considerable control over the content of material to be published. Utilizing this privilege, he has allowed some of our best material to be inserted in the product line of his normally conservative firm. He has justified this to management with a very subtle and admirable appeal, to their overdeveloped spirit of competition. Practically speaking, he has successfully maneuvered them into endorsing the secular adage "if it sells, print it!" His efforts have resulted in bringing together under the same roof the most liberal and the most conservative of theologians, an accomplishment which has escaped our ability to consummate for far too long. This has worked marvelously to confuse the church and those more immature disciples of the Enemy in particular. One of his greatest accomplishments was discontinuing a particularly annoying series of books pioneered by his firm, designed to defend the Enemy's so-called gospel against some of our more subtle efforts in the field of what the humans derisively refer to as "the world of the cults and the occult." We arranged for one of our prolific and sophisticated representatives in this cultic religious structure to approach him and launched our attack on a twofold perimeter. We suggested to him that a publishing house striving for international recognition should not be involved in publishing "negative" material about other people's religion.

Secondly, we dangled a large order from this organization before his greedy eyes. He could not resist the appeal to acquire a new status, and his conscience was salved by the prospect of increased revenues. There was only one point during the negotiation that even threatened our triumph, and that was when the Enemy's Spirit pricked his calloused soul. However, we overcame this by assuring him that he would be printing copies of the Enemy's Training Manual as a "positive" substitute for the "negative" defensive literature, and the victory was ours. It apparently did not occur to him that copies of the Enemy's Manual were already being printed worldwide by other of His agents, but at any rate we ended his firm's promotion of literature which was doing our Father's kingdom no good and indeed a great deal of harm. Unfortunately, another publishing house was led by the Enemy to take up where he left off, with even greater success in disrupting our activities, but our effort in the matter was not to be denied.

If you can expose your patient to some of these business ethics and somehow infect him with an ambition to succeed at the expense of his Christian principles, you will be well on the way to accomplishing our goals. It has been observed by one of the Enemy's better-known "disciples" that "the love of money is a root of all kinds of evils." This is, of course, quite true. But be certain that your patient is misdirected in this area too, so that he accepts the common cliché that it is not money that the humans love, not the thing in itself, but the comforts and conveniences and power that it commands.

Your patient must attach to his greed some type of rationalization or justification, and if it is based on the myth that he plans to use the money to better enable him to serve the Enemy's purposes, so much the better. Our long experience tells us that, with few notable exceptions, once the humans get control of money it has a peculiarly corrupting influence upon them. They conveniently forget their lofty initial motivation and plunge into satisfying their lusts and irrational whims.

I recall, in our last seminar at the College, the case of a renowned sinner who fled to the Enemy's camp and was filled with an admirable zeal (totally apart from knowledge) that led him to think that his great wealth should be used for the advancement of the Enemy's kingdom. His intentions were, of course, altruistic by all apparent standards, but we soon convinced him, as the Enemy prospered him, that a youthful dream should be fulfilled, and what better way to do so than with his increased monetary resources?

We reminded him of his boyhood desire to be a railroad engineer and prompted him to collect (of all things!) steam locomotives from all over the world. Next, we had him waste a substantial part of his wealth purchasing a large area of ground and creating a miniature railroad system with himself as chief engineer. He was photographed, dressed in an engineer's costume, sitting in the cab of one of his trains giving children free rides. Occasionally his conscience would be pricked about the matter and at such times he would undertake sorties into our Father's kingdom, converting not a small number of our armies to the Enemy's cause. I shudder to think what would have happened if such a dynamic and forceful human had been devoted solely to the Enemy's cause, and all the dollars we succeeded in diverting had been used as the Enemy intended in the invisible war. We suggested to him that by creating a state park for his "Christian railroad" untold thousands of children would relive their childhood dream of wanting to become railroad engineers. Through such suffocating nostalgia we effectively checkmated his considerable talents, thus causing his time to be dissipated in the childish pursuit of new locomotives rather than a greater number of souls. It apparently never occurred to him that the new generation of humans in the space age couldn't care less about railroad trains. Rockets and astronauts, yes, but old-fashioned locomotives? Decidedly not!

His timely death, at a relatively early age by earth calculations, left his financial empire in disarray, and he never did succeed in utilizing all his abilities and resources to resist us. Should your patient, therefore, succeed to great wealth, Wormwood, be sure to distract his attention with some kind of useless hobby. Get him to collecting things—anything, just so long as he spends his money for things other than the desires and aims of the Enemy. Keep him on the eternal treadmill of competition, excusing all the ruthless ethics and immoral practices of some twentieth-century Christian businessmen as just another means to the end of "glorifying" the Enemy. We know full well, of course, here in hell, that this involves the old chestnut of "the end justifies the means" or "let us do evil that good may come." But see to it that he doesn't know it, ever, and you will be amazed at the amount of money the Enemy intends for His purposes that we can channel to our own. It may be true that the cattle on a thousand hills belong to Him, but thanks to our efforts only a small percentage of them will ever get to any earthly slaughterhouse where it can do any of the human toads any good. When the man controls the money we are in danger, but when the money controls the man, then so can we, and the handwriting of his defeat is on the wall.

You have made a penetrating observation—that Christians appear to delight in the failure of their brothers to succeed, even in a task mutually beneficial to the Enemy's church as a whole. I never cease to marvel that they take a carnal satisfaction, traced no doubt to pernicious envy and jealousy, in difficulties and disasters which pursue other Christians with whom they are in competition. Naturally they parade pious hypocritical faces and intone sorrowful words over such debacles, but secretly we have taught them to feel good when others fail to perform, thus building up their own egos while tearing down those of their fellows. Some of them really think that they grow bigger because their co-workers suffer setbacks. Hopefully they will never find out that what injures one of them injures all of them and detracts from the Enemy's whole cause, since He considers them all members of some kind of a "body" where love and not competition is the final governing principle. We have not yet managed to penetrate His security cover enough to understand how this "love" functions, but we know that behind it all He has a selfish scheme and the poor fools are taken in by it. At the last our Father's dynamic realism will win out over all this, but in the meantime make the most of your patient's business opportunities and connections and be sure to neutralize his success and affluence by pointing it in the wrong direction. As ever,

> Your affectionate uncle,
> SCREWTAPE

Letter XIV

My Dear Wormwood:

It appears to me that you waste too many words on such comparatively trivial matters as sexual temptation. We all know that humans express themselves sexually in two primary ways: 1) that which we desire for them, and 2) the Enemy's rather parochial monogamous approach. I know, and we have discussed this before, that sex can be a powerful weapon on our side of the conflict; but it has distinct limitations, particularly if your patient ever comes to the realization that the record of history substantiates the validity of the Enemy's contention, i.e., that fidelity to one's mate is the foundation of social order. In short, marriage and the family are here to stay if the humans are entertaining any idea of remaining civilized.

There is hope in some areas, however, that the "new morality" with which they currently appear to be intoxicated may, in the name of "liberty and nondiscrimination," plant the seeds of their destruction and our conquest. It is a known fact, for instance, that the Enemy despises sexual actions contrary to what He has prescribed as the norm of conduct for mankind. We can, however, undermine a great deal of this by appealing to "fair play" and "equal rights" for everyone, regardless of sexual aberrations. Be extremely careful, however, of the word "depravity," the one word rapidly disappearing from the moral vocabulary and consciousness of this generation. Today loud cries are raised for the open acknowledgement that homosexuality is not an abnormality at all in human conduct, that there is indeed a "third sex," and that "consenting adults" should be permitted to indulge in any form of sexual behavior which gratifies their needs and does not infringe upon the activities of others. Hornswoggle informed me at our last council meeting that even certain medical practitioners who specialize in the study of the human psyche have boldly endorsed what was formerly sickness and aberration as an acceptable sexual phenomenon. I consider this to be one of our clearcut victories over the Enemy, whose attitude appears to be unchanging and puritanically annoying.

Your report indicates that your patient has been drawn into some of these controversies, not as a participant, to be sure, but because a local clergyman has "fearlessly" declared himself a homosexual and founded a church to further develop his fragmented interpretations of the Enemy's Training Manual. It is now proclaimed from the pulpit in the Enemy's name that "gay is good," a fact that their history alone refutes beyond question. In the apparently democratic cause of championing the right of the individual to do as he pleases, the obtuse humans are undercutting the very foundations of their civilization. Only a few of them have observed that if the Enemy intended individuals of the same sex to "love" each other, He would never have bothered creating male and female, a condition which alone guarantees the perpetuity of structured society. If we can once obscure the Enemy's intention from view, a total eclipse of His will may well be effected. If we can thus penetrate and influence the realms of education, government, the police, the military, and the clergy so that evil becomes good and good evil, all in the name of equal rights, we will have struck a telling blow to the Enemy's plan. If you can get your patient to subscribe to all or even some of this, the Enemy will at length have to apologize to Sodom and Gomorrah for His rather hasty actions, and we shall saddle homo sapiens with a homosexual holocaust unprecedented since the glorious libertine days of Greece and Rome. Gad, what a delicious prospect!

We must recognize that sexual temptation in itself holds very little interest for hell. In fact, our Father relegates its operation to second- and third-class tempters from the College. But the climate is right, and those who strenuously object we can still manage to label as "religious fanatics" or "puritanical" thinkers. That, by the way, is a very handy term simply because nobody ever stops to analyze it. Our Department of Philology has taken great pains to have the humans redefine this term so that, instead of meaning a high standard of morality, it refers to a narrow, bigoted, restraining frame of mind that can only be described by the worldly as "hypocritical."

The other issue which you raise for discussion, involving abortion, is a much more fertile field. Despite all of their vaunted knowledge of birth control, the humans, in their headlong attempt to achieve zero population growth (another new deity) have now been moved to consider abortion as a viable contraceptive device. Such reasoning regards the fetus as merely a lump of potentially valuable tissue. This can be extremely helpful to us because it tends to dehumanize them. If a woman can demand an abortion because "it is my body," it is only half a jump to euthanasia, which along the same line of logic ought also to be permitted for the benefit of those who consider themselves at the end of "my life and productivity." From that vantage point we can move handily to the elimination or liquidation, if you will, of the mentally handicapped and the hopelessly senile. After all, if the state can grant the right to abort life, why should it not appropriate the right to terminate it, in the supposed interest of an increasingly populous earth?

Our patients must be prevented from seeing the implications of their assent to unregulated abortion and homosexual practices as well, for if they once start to think instead of merely reacting, as we have carefully conditioned them to do for centuries, the game will be over.

This is not to say that the Enemy frowns on all abortion, for apparently He has made quite clear certain circumstances under which He permits it without penalty, and so the slogan "abortion is murder" can greatly facilitate our efforts when the issue is clouded and the Enemy's Training Manual is successfully distorted by fanatics on all sides of the controversy. Our interest is only in the confusion that the whole infantile business precipitates, so, if you can, do not hesitate to make it an issue in your patient's daily life.

Beyond all of the preceding considerations which we have mentioned, there is one area that the young tempter should study carefully and experiment with ceaselessly until it is refined to the fine science that our Father has managed to make it. I have reference to the subject of gluttony, which is far more deadly physically and spiritually than either homosexuality or untempered abortion. Christians who would never contemplate indulging in either practice are busily engaged in digging their own graves with knives and forks. In the broad spectrum of what one human has called diabetes desert and ulcer gulch there exists the ever-growing world of the gluttonous man and woman, victims of an affluent society that manages this ancient evil in the face of famine and starvation across half the earth.

Americans, particularly, contract this disease rather early, and make no mistake about it, it is a disease—of the soul, the mind, and the body. You state that your patient and his wife both overeat and that he remains thin, to her consternation, while she increases in girth. Herein lies a great truth about gluttony that is often overlooked, but nonetheless valid. The individual who eats more than he or she needs to in order to function effectively in society is a glutton. There are obese gluttons and there are thin gluttons. The former gives visible evidence in the padding of the body with excess fat. The latter conceals the evidence but pads the arteries with the same damaging substance.

We have largely managed to discredit those who have noticed this and insisted upon a return to "natural" foods and temperate eating habits, by caricaturing them as "faddists" or "health nuts." On the other side of the coin, we have persuaded many of those who are correct in their restraint at the table that anyone who disagrees with them is an ecological menace, a rivalry which generates an enormous amount of heat but, characteristically, very little if any light. The real fact of the matter is that gluttony is gluttony, regardless of the form it takes, and that Christians who shun transgression of the Enemy's law will abuse His temple with an overabundance of calories. Obviously this opens up a wide dimension for our activities since, for example, if we cannot cripple a minister's service for the Enemy, we can shorten his lifespan by encouraging him consistently to disobey the Enemy's counsel and allow himself to become a glutton. This is, in effect, self-destructive of his own capacity to serve the Enemy's kingdom, and He makes no promises to those who disobey its laws of nature, even if it be for His benefit. Wives are great allies to us in this area because they insist, in the name of "love," on both overfeeding and poorly feeding their husbands and households, not to mention neglecting their own diet regimen. Many a marriage that resisted our best attempts at dissipation on other fronts succumbed finally to gluttonous bulges in its participants' carcasses!

The final upshot of this entire rewarding human sin is the spectacle of hundreds of thousands of the Enemy's temples so clogged with the results of their dietary excesses that they mock His fruit of "self-control" and expose to devilish derision the concept of caring for His "temple." Personally speaking, I find gluttony, though tedious, to be a deadly and effective tool for leading the humans into temptation and seducing them to accelerated physical decay. One of the greatest evangelists in the Enemy's camp succumbed to gluttony after we had exhausted virtually every other approach to him. He was overfed wherever he went and used politeness as an excuse to literally eat himself to death. Another, known as the "Prince of Preachers," went down to defeat because, preach though he could (and with terrifying effect upon some of our best Tempters), he would not discipline himself to practice what he preached and failed to reach the Enemy's "threescore and ten" by almost two decades! One notable glutton of memory was inordinately proud of his family genealogy and coat of arms. Thanks to us, it underwent radical change and ended up as a crossed knife and fork over the lid of a garbage pail. If you need some pointers on the subject, I recommend a session with Munchsnacker, whose activities constantly supply us with juicy desserts on normally dull days.

Work hard, then, at generating caloric friction between your patient and his wife, never letting him know that they are both equally to blame and guilty of the same sin. This is a cruel jest on our part, to be sure, but one that is vindicated in its results by millions of premature Christian graves. True gluttons are made, not born, and there is a subtle pride about the whole disagreeable business. They love to seek out new palaces of gourmet delights, the "right" restaurants, the most "delicious" culinary sensations, the "in places" for those who appreciate the fine art of eating. Thank hell they don't see at the bottom of the whole thing that their stomachs are ruling their brains and that the Enemy created food for the purpose of sustaining life, not terminating it.

Let it not be forgotten that the Americans are a "diet-conscious" group of gluttons, who rush from one crash diet program to another, keeping two wardrobes in their closets to accommodate their everchanging shapes! It will do them no good, alas, to stuff themselves with vitamins, smear their wrinkled faces with hormone cream, exercise in their health spas, and jog over their streets and tracks unless they recognize (and we shall see to it that they do not!) that discipline over the body can be achieved only by those who are dedicated to a cause that can inspire self-control. Unfortunately, the Enemy has demonstrated a frustrating capacity to accomplish this if the creatures will obey Him. That practice, I might add, you must assist your patients to studiously avoid.

Enough, then, of the mundane homosexual and abortion methodology. Concentrate your efforts, if you must, on gluttony, since few can consistently resist it and there are those, evergrowing in number, who quite literally live to eat, and eat, and eat.

Your affectionate uncle,
SCREWTAPE

Letter XV

My Dear Wormwood:

From your last correspondence, I note that your patient is going in for a medical checkup due to some pains in his chest. I think it is important, therefore, that we discuss the subjects of fear and death as they generally affect mankind and your patient in particular.

From the perspective of experience, the human lice are certain of few changeless things during their dreary existence, but death is a notable exception. One of their number has stated that the living know they must die, and that it is fear of physical death that occupies and at length dominates the human soul. Now do not forget that fear can be a healthy attitude of mind providing it does not extend the knowledge of the Enemy; in fact, He has stated that fear of Him is the beginning of wisdom. Your patient is just now fearful about his health, so see to it that his agnostic physician calms that fear, lest he begin to think of death and inevitably of meeting the Enemy. We can tolerate and even encourage all types of fears, such as the fear of one man or nation for another or the fear of insanity, poverty,

persecution, sickness, suffering, death, and even fear of us!
But you must never allow the specter of fear of the Enemy
to attract or hold your patient's attention. Fear, as has been
observed, produces torment because it creates anxiety, and
anxiety creates doubt, and doubt is the father of sin.

The human's fear of death can be exploited primarily
because it must be experienced to be understood. Since
they cannot do so on a personal or individual level without
leaving the dimension of earth, what is unknown to them is
to be feared.

There are two excellent ways to cope with your patient's
exposure to fear of death. The first is to convince him that
death is inevitable, and the second that it is natural for
everyone to die. Suggest to him that even the Enemy's
Training Manual teaches that "it is given to all men once to
die," but make sure you omit the unfortunate sentence that
follows that quotation, which alludes to that coming judgment. One of the worst things in the world is to have your
patient become aware of the fact that the Enemy has
promised to judge the entire universe and, since he forms a
part of it, it becomes a fearful, impending threat.

If you can persuade him (as we have a large segment of
the psychiatrists and psychologists of earth) that these two
things are true, he will have missed the whole point that the
Enemy through physical death is trying to make. We know,
of course, that death may not be inevitable, nor is it natural
to man. It may not be inevitable for all men because the
Enemy says He intends to preserve some of his so-called
"flock" alive until He establishes His kingdom. Our Father
strenuously rejects this idea, but so far we have hindered
but not been able to abort the Enemy's efforts. Further
than this, it certainly is not natural for man to die, because
the Enemy designed him for a "natural" life of immortal
fellowship with Himself—a dream, I might add, which our
Father turned into a nightmare in Eden! However, so long
as you can keep these facts from him, he will begin to

accept the inevitability of death and the fact that it is "perfectly natural." Fear, it should be observed, is a very real form of bondage—a bondage which our Father exercised over the entire human race, beginning with the fall in Eden and unhappily terminating at the totally unanticipated resuscitation of His Chief Emissary in an obscure Palestinian garden a few millennia ago.

Despite this unfortunate event, a great majority of mankind are still in a voluntary bondage to the fear of death, and good use can be made of this kind of fear at times. I well remember one of my own patients a few centuries ago who became terrified of death and was so obsessed by fear that he began to become extremely religious! This, of course, was an intolerable situation. So I suggested to him that rather than worry about the inevitable and the natural he should enjoy himself today while he still could and take no thought for what would occur tomorrow. He accepted this suggestion as a perfectly logical course of action and plunged into a life of debauchery almost unparalleled in my experience as a tempter. He consoled himself with the idea that at the last moment he would repent and throw himself upon the mercy of the Enemy—a most helpful delusion we have sustained for centuries. But since it is the Enemy who determines the opportunity for repentance, and not the will of man, our Father's house below overflows.

We have also had remarkable success among the medical profession, particularly some Viennese psychiatrists and their disciples, through implanting the idea that fear and its twin sister, guilt, are evils to be exorcised while lying on the psychiatrist's sofa—an occasion, I might observe, for shrinkage of the patient's pocketbook along with the mind! Hell knows that both fear and guilt can be instructive or destructive, depending upon its context. But your patient must not notice this. It is quite healthy and indeed wise for the humans to be afraid of lightning and radiation and, as the Enemy has observed, it is in their best interests to feel guilty when they have transgressed His law. But so long as they are content to brand all fear and all guilt as demons to be "exorcised" (forgive the expression), our patients are in no real danger from fear of the Enemy and His justice.

As an aside, I might add that we received tremendous assistance in the area of reducing the humans' fear of death from, of all places, the undertaking profession. The "merchants of death," as they have been referred to by one of the humans, have perfected the cosmetology of embalming to a degree undreamed-of in past centuries. They have done their level best to pull the fang or, if you will, the sting of death by turning mortuaries into "slumber parlors," and through the adept usage of cotton and cosmetics they have made human corpses into models of modern taxidermy. Indeed, it is not uncommon to hear humans refer to a deceased relative or friend as "never looking better" while in his or her coffin! They have also performed an invaluable service for us by removing the funeral service from the church, where those who attend the service might be exposed to the real truth about death and their need to face both their fear and its reality on a one-to-one basis.

Christian undertakers are perhaps the one exception to this observation, since many of them insist upon intruding their devotion to the Enemy and His message into the normally depressing business of burial. But unfortunately the profit motive extends not only to the unbeliever but to the believer as well, and sometimes even they succumb to the temptation to make death less than what it truly is. Your patient must never, never learn under any circumstances that death is not the friend of man but his enemy—in fact, the last enemy to be destroyed—and that the Enemy did not place His church on earth in order to suffer martyrdom or to long for death but rather to proclaim His message and resist us. The grand illusion is to convince our patients that death is a natural friend of man, a fact that agitates the Enemy no end. The Enemy's Training Manual goes to great lengths to point out that His love "casts out fear" and that death itself will inevitably be swallowed up by life in His projected victory over our Father below. This is, of course, all nonsensical, but if your patient begins to really comprehend it, you are in for real difficulty. If the humans ever discover that there is a fear that is "clean," if they ever discover that they are not to be afraid of our Father below but rather of Him who is able to cast both soul and body into eternal fire, and if they ever learn that hell was designed for us and not for them, matters will be complicated far beyond anything you have ever imagined.

There are two principal ways that the fear of death may be dispelled. The first is by deception and the second by revelation. Those who have rejected the Enemy's way of what He calls "salvation" frequently overcome fear of death by asserting that it does not really exist at all. One simply goes on into a state of eternal progression or reincarnation (one of our most useful methods). We have encouraged this viewpoint by frequent appearances at séances, where the performances given by some of our colleagues representing themselves as "departed spirits from earth" would win an academy award in any production that Hollywood ever designed. From such encounters the humans have wrongly inferred that all departed spirits inevitably go to the same place; that is, good spirits enter the presence of the Enemy and bad spirits are purged until they are made acceptable to the Enemy.

This acceptance is conditioned upon their works and/or suffering in the upward scale of progression, a great victory for us no matter what. We have managed to convince a great mass of mankind that they can accomplish for themselves what the Enemy failed to accomplish by His absurd insistence upon the efficacy of that cross. But be that as it may, it is an effective tool. The second method is repugnant to us, and I am not of the temperament to discuss it at great length; however, the Enemy makes the representation to humans that He has revealed to them an eternal truth—that those who are willing to cast themselves without reservation upon His mercy (an empty assertion at best) will enter immediately upon the death of their physical form into His presence. As one of His apostles most cogently put it, "I desire the departing and the being with (   ),° which is far better." This troublesome fellow also "revealed" the Enemy's plan to resurrect and recreate the humans in His own image in what is termed a "glorified body." We, of course, recognize that such claims are fantasy, and you had better see to it that your patient does not give them serious consideration. Whatever you do, whenever your patient reflects on death, remind him it is a long, long way off; that it is an unpleasant thought and should not be considered seriously at the moment. Never let him learn that the Enemy knows how to deliver the godly out of temptation and to keep the ungodly under punishment.

It is an unfortunate fact that the Enemy's so-called "love" does indeed appear to cast out fear and that His promise of absolution for guilt even at the last moment has been kept a disturbing number of times. Learn from all of this, Wormwood, that the humans are a natural prey to fear and that they must not learn that our Father below has been deprived of the power of death. For those who obey the Enemy, it is rumored to be but a valley of shadows paradoxically illuminated by the One who passed through it both ways, the One of whom it is said He lives that death may die.

In the end, though, we shall be the conquerors in this conflict, because if the wages of sin is death, the Enemy has made a poor showing of preserving mankind from its effects. Make no mistake, the final victory will be ours!

Your affectionate uncle,
SCREWTAPE

° *Title deleted*

Letter XVI

My Dear Wormwood:

There are times when I wonder what is happening to our young tempters under Slubgob's leadership. I have always been opposed to crash programs, and your naiveté is obviously sound evidence that I am correct.

You write that your patient has discovered the world of the occult, and thereby the real possibility of your existence. You say that he is even fearful that he may be under our surveillance if not our outright attack. First, remember that you must not become unduly alarmed; this can be handled in many ways quite successfully. Keep in mind that speed and misdirection are of the essence. The patient should be put in touch with someone who specializes in debunking the so-called world of the occult. A sound agnostic or skeptic can be of real value to us here, since he will undertake to prove to your patient that certain inept mediums, fortune-tellers, and assorted occultic quacks are charlatans and frauds.

I remember that toward the end of my own modestly

illustrious career I utilized a famous magician to "unmask" (as he put it) and disprove "all supernatural forces in the occult." Naturally we never let him catch the scent of our real power, and in its absense he was quite successful in convincing millions that we do not exist. He became a convert, however, at the time of his death and made a tasty morsel for many a hungry young tempter below!

We have always had rather splendid results, historically, with skeptics and agnostics. The one believes that nothing can be certain at all, except of course what he is certain of, and the other that nothing can ever really be finally known except the knowledge which he possesses. Both seem blissfully unaware of the contradictions involved in both positions and continue to pose as champions of logical thought. See that such valued allies are encouraged wherever possible, along with liberal clergymen who, clothed in all the outward credentials of the church (which your patient has come to respect), will undercut his belief in our power and explain away his apprehensions as "Freudian guilt" and "childhood fears."

Should your patient, however, find the antisupernatural approach untenable (and the Enemy will be busy about this, you may be sure), some Satanic shock therapy may have rewarding results. Stimulate his curiosity to the point that he grows inquisitive about our activities and power. Since humans are prone to ignore the warnings given in the Enemy's Training Manual concerning the dangers of exploring our realm (and make no mistake—the real occult is all ours), he may be betrayed by his own ignorance. Keep foremost in your mind that human nature is addicted to probing the future, ever learning but never able to quite lift the veil that separates time and eternity. Throughout their history we have been able to utilize everything, from astrology to witchcraft, as a means of encouraging their vain quest.

We have consequently sponsored séances, cast

horoscopes, levitated tables, "fulfilled" predictions, and even duplicated the "miraculous." What a gamut of deviltry we have run to substitute experience for revelation and fraud for fact!

Your patient, then, can be tantalized by the "unknown" and dazzled by supposed glimpses of the future in what is really a pathetic search for security and power. He must never learn that real supernatural power is not displayed in such parlor tricks and that the only security he can ever have is a gift from the Enemy. But you must not allow him to even suspect this.

Your patient must be driven inevitably to one of two extremes. He must reject our existence (now an unlikely possibility, due to your lack of perception) or he must recognize that, while we do exist, we need only be feared by those who are truly evil. We must (ever so subtly, to be sure) lead him to a "live and let live" philosophy where we are concerned. We have perfected this in many primitive cultures, where we have convinced them the Enemy is *not* to be feared because of His supposed benevolence, whereas we *are* to be feared and even placated because of our malevolence. But progress of this kind in your patient's case will take time, although we are making real gains toward its general acceptance of late. Your patient must never learn that evil is evil regardless of its magnitude. But it serves our ends to let him think that we are only concerned with gross evil, whereas the Enemy views all of it with His usual narrow hostility.

In view of these facts, then, I would suggest that you arrange to have your patient exposed (though not overly so) to some radical sermons, books, and films on the subject of Satanic power, particularly our capacity to possess humans. Now we know he cannot be possessed, due to the Enemy's stringent restrictions and His petulant occupancy of what He calls "His temple." But your patient is by no means sure of this fact, so if you cannot convince him, confuse him with fear and uncertainty, the twin high priests of indecision.

Fortunately for our cause, there are a number of the Enemy's well-intentioned but poorly informed servants who can be recruited to assist us at this point. Your patient's ignorance of the Enemy's Training Manual will be invaluable. By incessantly warning the patient about us (they even credit us with the ability to possess him!) they will frighten and shock him to the place where he will avoid rather than resist us.

Another service they render us is to shift responsibility for his sins from himself to us, so that his carnal nature is allowed to function unfettered by spiritual restraints. In this manner your patient is taught to blame everything on us, thus muting his own conscience and personal guilt.

At every turn we must make certain, then, that demonology is substituted for carnality. The more he makes us his scapegoat, the less we need to worry about his repentance. See to it that the waters of his mind remain continuously muddy concerning our existence and the extent of our power, and his future will grow deliciously darker day by day.

> Your affectionate uncle,
> SCREWTAPE

Letter XVII

My Dear Wormwood:

I feel constrained to tell you that you are overlooking a great opportunity to make use of your patient's interest in furthering his education. The pursuit of education for the purpose of directing his energies away from the service of the Enemy must be one of our prime considerations, just as education for the sake of education has been the watchword in our secular emphasis for the last 75 years. It makes no real difference to us who is educated, just so long as we are able to manipulate both the means and the ends. It has been one of our most soundly demonstrated propositions that if you educate a thief you only increase his capacity to steal. So if the unregenerate become educated it will increase their capacity to be of service to our Father's cause, since a trained intellect dedicated to our goals can only extend our influence among the humans.

We have also succeeded in convincing many of them that education in itself can cure what the Enemy imperiously designates as the "wages of sin." We have, with meticulous care, succeeded in establishing the fantasy that all crimes and social and political inequities, as well as the poverty, injustice, and exploitation which exist in the world, are primarily the result of a lack of education, combined with the influence of environment. Education has become one of the grand panaceas of hell, applicable to almost all situations on earth where the "have nots" think it will gain for them what the "haves" presently enjoy. We can be grateful that they learn very little from experience, for if they once grasp the truth that education may shape the mind but does not shape the soul—in fact is neutral where spiritual values are concerned except under our superior guidance—we shall have to find a new tool.

Where your patient is concerned, further education can cause him to question some of his own values and, more important, those of the Enemy. To this end, some basic courses in sociology, psychology, and, by all means, philosophy will help prepare the way quite adequately. Through the systematic influence of our Propaganda Division and its brilliant director, Tallbrow, those three fields have been successfully infiltrated by many of our representatives, who have thoroughly secularized the entire structure of thinking in these disciplines worldwide. With few exceptions we have translated sociology to refer primarily to environment, human social behavior, and statistical trends which allegedly analyze and predict what is likely to happen under almost any projected circumstances.

We have so befuddled the sociologists with a mass of contradictory data that they have largely evolved into a frustrated group of vague thinkers who rarely speak in verifiable specifics, and instead delight in banal generalities. Most of them are answering questions that no practical person is any longer asking and are attempting to explain away the obvious depravity of man on the basis of his socioeconomic involvement with environment and change. With few exceptions they have largely ignored any really scientific analysis of society (though they love to refer to themselves as scientists) and have settled for the mediocrity of social physicians who observe and treat the symptoms of a disease without the slightest knowledge of what causes it. If they ever come to the place of recognizing the humans' rebellion against the Enemy's law as the greatest single common denominator toward understanding the behavior of mankind, we could encounter real problems. Pragmatically speaking, this is highly unlikely because, even if they discover the real cause, we have programmed them to think that obedience to the Enemy is an incursion upon their freedoms, so they will most likely ignore even those concrete findings.

Should your patient not respond to the sociological influence and become disenchanted with the statistical boredom that ensues, there is always the merry-go-round of modern psychology. Try, whenever possible, to have him come in contact with those pseudo-intellectuals who frequent university corridorsand lecture halls, confident that a little learning is *not* a dangerous thing. In such an agnostic atmosphere (further sterilized by a competent atheistic instructor) your patient will be cowed into silence by his own lack of knowledge and will hopefully begin to succumb to the "psychological explanations" of not only his religious conviction but also of his conversion and commitment to the Enemy. Direct his thoughts to that old Satanic dodge that men believe because they have created a god in their own likeness and worship Him because they are afraid both to die and to face the problems of living. Help him to think of all of this as "bold" and "intellectually satisfying."

Should any of his Christian friends call those views into question, remind him of his intellectual superiority and newly gained knowledge. Guide him so that he begins to see the Enemy as the object of his "wish to believe" (oh, how useful this concept has been to us!) and then suggest to him that the Enemy cannot really exist at all, since He is only the "wish fulfillment" of man's desire to be immortal and to survive the death of his body. Keep the solution to this fabulous fallacy always beyond the reach of his budding intellectual fingers. He must not discover that a man's *desire to believe* in the existence of the Enemy cannot be legitimately cited as proof of the Enemy's *nonexistence* any more than *a desire or a wish* for the coming of dawn after suffering a night of pain can be cited as proof that dawn will *not* arrive! Such a logical answer will forever elude him, and he will happily embrace the foregoing error now deified by most agnostic psychologists. But remember, we will be successful in this approach only as long as we encourage him to merely react to, rather than to think through, such challenges to his faith.

If all else should fail you in the intellectual maelstrom, there is always philosophy. By its very definition it is the pursuit and love of human wisdom, and indeed many august and brilliant personages have trod its pathways over the centuries. Stimulate his interest in the great minds that have thought through the perennial problems of life without arriving at *final* solutions, and introduce him to the generally agnostic and skeptical attitude of the philosophers which passes for genius and should provide a model for his own attitude of inquiry. See to it, if at all possible, that he becomes so awed by the worldly wisdom of his instructor that he does not recognize the shift in his thinking from the authority of the Enemy and His Word to the quicksand of human logic and reasoning processes. Concentrate upon creating within him a skeptical attitude toward everything under the guise of being "empirical and scientific" about life. If you manage it properly he will not notice that the skeptic who maintains that it is unscientific and illogical to believe anything absolutely himself violates logical thought by insisting that skepticism must be believed absolutely.

This is a patent contradiction if ever there was one! One

philosopher has even suggested that empiricism carried to its logical conclusion becomes empiricide because one seeks to prove too much from scientific methodology and human experience, to the point that all reality, including emotion, thought, and history itself must be sacrificed on the agnostic altar of allegedly infallible inquiry.

Given enough time, the philosophers will lead your patient a merry and totally unrewarding chase in his quest for "truth," and, as long as this can be maintained, his mind will be diverted from his relationship to the Enemy. Do not allow him to examine the record of philosophers so far as the translation of their theories about life and its values into the practical realm of coping with the problems of life and its values are concerned, or all your efforts will at that moment come to naught. Should he uncover the truth that the philosophers are, in fact, the drones of history who have contributed overall very little to mankind and a great deal to our Father's cause, he might see that, while mouthing great platitudes about brotherhood, charity, aesthetics, and morality, philosophers have been notably deficient in these virtues themselves.

Need I remind you of Nietzsche and Marx, two splendid examples whose disciples (Hitler and Lenin) nearly succeeded in wiping out the whole race of human vermin— now that is practical application with a vengeance! What they have succeeded in doing is to consistently refute each other, confuse their constituencies, and cloud the issues our Enemy deems important. It is a sad commentary, but nonetheless true, that the philosophers have not built the hospitals, educational institutions, and charitable institutions of earth which are a blight on our Father's kingdom. The Enemy's servants have been remarkably successful wherethe philosophers have failed, so keep your patient's mind occupied with what they are *saying* in philosophy, *not* what they have *done*. As long as he is busy trying to solve "the problem of evil" or "absolute truth versus relativism" he will not notice that the great god logic really proves nothing at all, that ethics and morality are rooted in the Enemy and His insistence upon "love," and that some things just cannot be solved because the humans' mind is limited and incapable of assimilating data with which we are well acquainted.

Channel his thinking particularly, then, to these areas of education. Lead him to believe that all truth must be scientifically and inductively demonstrated, and massage his ego and superior sense of accomplishment at every opportunity. While education, when dedicated to the Enemy, can be a terrible force toward the advancement of His kingdom, we have the greater advantage because He demands that it be consecrated to Him in order for it to become effective in the lives of His servants. Our Father, however, recognizes it for what it truly is—an opportunity to deceive, if possible, the most sincere and devout, who fail to recognize its limitations and pitfalls.

Your affectionate uncle,
Screwtape

Letter XVIII

My Dear Wormwood:

Your patient appears to be making good progress on his downward journey, and, best of all, he is enjoying it! There is no doubt that the Enemy will attempt to rescue him, but even He has His limitations, and you will do well to refresh your memory about them.

From our own very detailed studies we have observed that He cannot change, cannot fail to be truthful, cannot forsake His servants, and cannot forgive what He calls blasphemy of His Spirit. Further than this, He cannot fail His Word or fail to redeem sinners apart from that primitive cross which stubbornly resists all our best efforts to obscure. The Enemy cannot do any of these and other lesser things because His inscrutable nature prohibits it. But these are not factors open to exploitation; however, the following are, and directly concern your patient.

Keep uppermost in your mind that your patient possesses within his own being the most powerful means at our disposal to limit the Enemy and His activities. As our

Father below has often pointed out, when the Enemy decided to bestow freedom of choice upon creation He ran the risk of creation not being willing to subject itself to His tyrannical control, a truth amply demonstrated by our rebellion and, later, that of Adam's race. Men, therefore, possess the means to limit the Enemy because He has granted it to them (we would never have made that mistake!) and such an opportunity must not be neglected by any truly dedicated tempter.

The first and most common means of limiting the Enemy is by causing His servants to distrust Him or, in a word, to prompt them to doubt and unbelief. When the Enemy walked the earth in the form of the two-legged barbarians, even He at times could work no great works or miracles because of the unbelief of the very people He had entered the world to redeem. The first members of the human family lost their admittedly exalted estate because of unbelief, and the Enemy has made its diametric opposite (which he calls faith) the sole means whereby man may come to experience Him. In point of fact, without it He deems it impossible to even approach His presence.

It was unbelief, one of our most versatile methods, that limited His chosen people from entering Canaan, unbelief that destroyed their first king, and finally unbelief that impaled Him on a tree. The specter of unbelief caused His disciples to reject His resurrection and has been a perpetual curse upon His church to the present day. It is apparent, then, that the more effectively we persuade man *not* to trust Him, the more decisively we limit His power. It is paradoxical indeed, if not directly contradictory, that He who claims omnipotence should permit its antithesis (personal limitation) to exist. This has led our Father to the brilliant conclusion that He is not all-powerful at all, but simply maintains the appearance of such in order to frighten us into believing that absurd tale of a final judgment and our ultimate overthrow. In the end it will be our unbelief which will limit Him and hobble His hosts so that He will be forced to come to terms.

A second and more subtle way of placing limitations upon the Enemy is by seeing to it that your patient does not grow spiritually, so that as a carnal or immature Christian he never grows up to the full stature of spiritual manhood that will enable him to resist us and fulfill the Enemy's plan for his life. I well recall, at Corinth, when that persistent agitator, Paul, was on the scene, how clearly he saw through our designs and assailed our three primary tactics—division, envy, and strife. To this day his writings on the subject are a continuous thorn in what would be called our Father's "flesh," if indeed He had any.

The Enemy has as His goal the perfecting or, as He puts it, the maturing of His servants so that they defeat the curse of spiritual childhood by growing in His grace and thereby growing up. This can be thwarted by convincing your patient that reading the Bible and going to church is a sufficient means of assuring spiritual growth. Be vigilant lest the Enemy's Spirit point out to him that receiving the Enemy is one thing but walking with Him is another! It is by this process of walking in fellowship with Him that the Enemy plans to establish and ground your patient in his faith. This enables His disciples not to set their sights upon earthly goals, which are transient at best. We may succeed in limiting the Enemy here if we encourage the patient to be content with the first principles of the "good news," which is described as milk, while depriving him of any real incentive toward an appetite for the meat of the Enemy's message. If you can keep him in perpetual childhood, the limitation of the Enemy can be maintained indefinitely.

You have already mentioned in your last correspondence the possibility of limiting the Enemy by causing your patient to fail in his obligations as they are expressed in the Enemy's Word. I heartily concur that this certainly curtails His power. How happily I recall His anger when that flea-bitten tribe of sluggish Semites He delivered from us in Egypt failed to maintain their covenants with Him. It restrained Him from blessing them and, indeed, became responsible for their most serious judgment, a forty-year trek in the desert. Time and again it has been demonstrated that our patients limit the Enemy most decisively when they disobey His express wishes through ignorance, selfishness, or pride and thereby prevent Him from rewarding them and providing for their needs.

How often the Enemy has wanted to act positively in behalf of His children, only to have them mock His alleged omnipotence and provide us with limitless delight at His all-too-apparent frustration. It is undeniable that, in the economy of the Enemy, that which He designates as "sin" interrupts and interferes with the fellowship He dotes on with His disciples. The surest way to maintain that hostility on His part toward their infractions of His will is to discourage them from repentance. This is the only action that can pave the way for their restoration and, in turn, release Him from this limitation. Repentance, by the way, simply refers to a reversal of course in the mind or the thinking processes. But one of our great triumphs has been to confuse it with penance, which is nothing more than self-effort to make up with works what can only be remedied by faith and spiritual restraint. If we can keep them thinking in this vein, even the gift of salvation itself can be undermined, since the Enemy vigorously insists that it be by grace, undiluted by human works. Penance works, and if we can coat it with the veneer of piety it will serve us all the better.

I recognize, as you reflect on these things and attempt to apply them in the life of your patient, that some of the older and more outmoded methods still taught at the College may interfere with your judgment. Let me assure you that some of the most mature tempters to have graced the pages of *Who's Who in Hell* acknowledge my pioneer activities in establishing these principles. As far as I am concerned, then, limiting the Enemy is not fun and games; it is necessary to our survival in the tempter's arena. If you young fiends are unwilling to learn by the experiences of others more qualified, don't come crawling to me when the Enemy pulls some of your fangs! Then, in the words of our Father below, you can go to heaven!

> Your affectionate uncle,
> SCREWTAPE

Letter XIX

My Dear Wormwood:

It is not only tiring but exasperating to expect a detailed report from you and to receive instead what can only be described as incompetent ramblings! We have been all through the matter of temptation on a domestic level, but it appears you still need some pointers in this category. First of all, it is fortunate for our cause that your patient has been delinquent in his church attendance of late and has failed to pray and read the Enemy's Training Manual with his wife. This lapse of fidelity has led him into a spiritual depression or doldrum and a period of discouragement. He must be kept in this superb condition as long as possible because, if he does not draw near to the Enemy in repentance, the Enemy will refuse to draw near to him and the field is open wide for our exploitation.

It is also all to our benefit that he is taking home his frustrations at the office and then taking them out on his wife and children. From what you tell me of his wife, she is not the "Job type" (as our Father refers to it) and is more than likely to praise and thank the Enemy for the trial of their faith than to reproach Him or nag her husband. To offset her unreasonably chaste and self-controlled spirit, encourage your patient to pick at her, to criticize whatever she does, and to speak harshly to the children. Have him blame her for his problems, and remind him of the now-forsaken glories of his bachelorhood amidst the absence of marital and parental responsibilities.

Her mother may markedly assist you in realizing this goal because she is a first-rate status seeker in nominal attendance at a fashionable liberal church and a dedicated devotee of social position and material wealth. I have instructed Snobsnivel to give you assistance here, due to his admitted expertise amongst this type. She is particularly distraught that her daughter has "married beneath her station" and looks upon the interest your patient's wife has in the things of the Enemy as "religious fanaticism" and "potentially damaging to our family's image in the community."

Though a secret racist, she hypocritically supports the NAACP, CORE, and other minority groups but in reality despises them all; she particularly dislikes black people, whom she would like to see returned to Africa as rapidly as possible so that America could once more be "for the Americans." Such a fine specimen of our propaganda should not be neglected, and we have enrolled her as an honorary charter member in Hell's chapter of S.P.O.N.G.E. (Society for the Prevention of Negroes Getting Everything). She is a perfect dupe, who cannot see the inconsistencies of her own positions, no matter how clearly her longsuffering husband, daughter, and son-in-law have patiently tried to point them out to her. I understand that she has much the same attitude toward the American Indians, confusing their reception of her Pilgrim ancestors with Custer's Last Stand. This can only be adequately described, even by our standards, as fractured history.

You must see to it that she maintains her crusade to dominate her daughter's home and life in the interest of enlightened social climbing. Be sure to have her countermand parental authority in your patient's home by doting on her grandchildren and insisting that they have all the "finer advantages and benefits" her position can afford. This is a proven way of stirring up contention between your patient and his wife, because instinctively she will be called upon to defend her mother on that basis alone, a real advantage for us that you must not fail to seize.

It is important to note that the Enemy will doubtless counterattack, capitalizing on His "right" to the ownership of their souls and attempting to reinstitute what has become known in heavenly circles as "the family altar." Upon that altar He desires that they consecrate themselves as holy and acceptable "living sacrifices," which He deems their reasonable service. But we have seen to it that many such living sacrifices have successfully squirmed off His altar and are briskly walking in the wide worldly path which our Father has so ingeniously designed. Your patient must not come to the awareness that the Enemy wishes to be his constant companion and that only his own perversity and sin prevent this. Family altars can be devastating to our very best assaults because the family that is united in prayer to the Enemy and in praise to Him assures His certain intervention and our ultimate frustration.

One of the most successful instances that I can recall of our disruption of family life occurred in the home of one of the Enemy's devoted disciples, a type not unlike that of your patient. This man was converted from great evil; in fact he was a most useful tool of ours until the Enemy confronted him one day with the reality of eternal loss, and years of our efforts were demolished in minutes. Upon his conversion he diligently studied the Enemy's Training Manual, opened his soul to His Spirit, and became a dynamic force in the kingdom above. But all was not lost, for his newfound zeal was, alas, without sufficient knowledge, and, being a highly emotional person, he slowly but surely began to ground his conversion on his feelings and not on what the enemy did and said. He felt it his bound duty to "evangelize" everyone with whom he came in contact and became such a self-righteous, Pharisaical bore that many humans who might otherwise have listened to him were repulsed by his attitude and tactics. One of his great deficiencies which we noted was his inability to submit to authority, coupled with an unteachable spirit.

Inevitably we pressured him into questioning his conversion by the simple device of having him feel "saved" one day and lost the next. We convinced him that the essence of the Christian life was striving for the production of spiritual fruit, which, as you well know, does not grow because of human effort, however strenuous and devoted, but through yieldedness to the Spirit of the Enemy. It was not long before we had him entrapped in one of the oldest of all errors, that of being saved by grace and kept by works.

What a magnificent specimen he finally became— neglecting his family to run hither and yon directed, he thought, by the Enemy's Spirit, but in reality by his own desire to generate spiritual fruit and to be influential. It never occurred to him that holiness, as the Enemy defines it, is bestowed upon those who rest in what He has promised, not in their own vain strivings. Today his home is broken, his wife is alienated by his legalistic inconsistencies and pseudo-holiness, and his children are confused by a father whose actions spoke so loud they could not hear what he was saying. The man began with the very best of intentions but rested upon his feelings and not upon the Enemy's Word—something you must strive to have your patient emulate. Incidentally, the Enemy, oddly enough, did not forsake him even when he was led by some of our experienced Lechers into the grossest of sins and worldly practices. But instead that alien Spirit drove him at length to repentance, doubtless because of the heavenly seed planted within him. Today, despite some of our strongest assaults, he appears to be gaining ground, and, unless we can prevent it, he will soon be most certainly restored to his wife and to fellowship in his church. I cite this not as an instance of our failure (we still have hopes for some new approaches the College has suggested) but to remind you that it must not occur in the case of your patient.

Finally, I must draw your attention to one of the Enemy's oldest tactics, lest its simplicity lull you into a false sense of security. I refer to the subject of praise and thanksgiving, which I find personally nauseating and absolute proof of His egocentricity. Be that as it may, we have not as yet been able to comprehend what He is really up to in the whole matter, but what must concern us is its almost miraculous effectiveness. According to the Enemy, He is still willing to accept some kinds of sacrifices, such as a dedicated life, good works, generosity to the poor and unfortunate, and the giving of thanks. However, the most dangerous of them all (to us) is the sacrifice of praise. The Enemy is convinced because of the mere fact that He created men and angels that He is entitled to their love and praise. He has attached great significance to the latter and blesses out of all reasonable proportion those who practice it. Naturally, we who are enlightened are not about to participate in what our Father describes as "an orgy of egotism." However, when His disciples do exercise their prerogative of praise to worship, thank, and glorify Him He responds with alarming rapidity.

I well remember one instance which stands out above all others in my experience. We had worked for literally months to cripple the Christian walk of a prominent and promising member of one of the Enemy's congregations. We succeeded in having his wealthy in-laws spoil and then alienate his wife with gifts and material comforts which he was unable to provide. We next saw to it that his stature was diminished in her eyes by the loss of his job and his seeming inability to get another one. His wife eventually left him and went to live with her parents, and his financial obligations reached such a stage of decay that he was contemplating suicide. My, how we strove to get him to take that last step. You know the technique ("nobody loves you, nobody cares for you, all hope is gone, God has forsaken you,"etc., etc.).

Well, we almost managed it, until a visiting clergyman suggested what to us was an incredible solution. This meddling dolt knelt down with him and began to praise and thank the Enemy for the time of testing through which he was passing. I tell you it was unendurable the way they went on praising and thanking Him for His mercy, compassion, and promised faithfulness. The more we attempted to penetrate with the stark realism of his hopeless situation, the louder grew the echoes of praise, until finally we had to break off the attack. Needless to say, the Enemy quickly responded with a new job and restored his wife and child with stunning suddenness. Even his in-laws (our most trusted allies in the matter) were awed by the fact that his salary was almost doubled and his obligations fulfilled to everyone's satisfaction. Today he is extremely difficult for us to reach because at the first sign of our presence he falls to his knees and calls on the Enemy. The sound of those noxious prayers and reverent ramblings quenches all the din and fury of hell with a maddening peace that quite frankly surpasses even our superior understanding.

There is one way, however, that intolerable situations of this nature may be avoided. The Enemy's Training Manual suggests that in all circumstances His servants are to give thanks. That is, in the midst of the worst possible occurrences they are, in effect, to trust Him, doubting nothing. They are to believe that He will use all situations to work out everything for good to those who love Him, to those whom He has summoned according to some inscrutable purpose. To undercut all this fanciful and unprofitable conjecture, our Linguistic Department has come up with a devilishly clever solution. We have persuaded not a small number of the Enemy's disciples to misinterpret what He means when He encourages them to "give thanks." We have placed the emphasis in their minds that the phrase "*in* everything give thanks" really means "*for* everything give thanks." This beautiful tactic has resulted in many of the Enemy's disciples thanking Him for all the misfortunes which overtake them, all the diseases which afflict them, and all the circumstances which oppress them, oblivious to the fact that we, not He, are the source of their trials and tribulations. They have forgotten that the Enemy tempts no one and that therefore their trials and temptations are not *created* by Him but are rather *permitted* by Him as a means of refining their faith. We must keep them from discovering that what the Enemy really said was that no matter what condition they find themselves in, they are in the midst of it to offer thanks and praise, an action which constitutes an affirmation of their confidence in Him despite the difficulties of the moment. Discovery of this truth about the Enemy's behavior creates far too many problems than the encounter is worth, so don't let it happen!

Your comment on prayer itself is one with which I heartily agree. We certainly must keep them believing that "prayer changes things." If we once communicate this successfully to the humans, we will have caricatured the Enemy as a changeable being, subject to the will and whim of the creature rather than remaining sovereign as the Creator. It is obvious that if the Enemy is infinite (an unproven assertion which our Father challenges!) then nothing can take Him by surprise. All human reasoning, then, is simply an exercise of the freedom of choice and is part and parcel of His whole fantastic myth about love and responsibility. It is a fact, of course (challenged by few informed devils), that the Enemy introduced prayer as a means of communication between Himself and the humans for the purpose of voluntarily bringing their wills into harmony with His own. By this process it is they who alter their wishes to conform to His will, on the totally unreasonable ground that He always knows what is best for His servants. Continue, then, to foster the idea of the Enemy as a capricious Deity, capable of being swayed and influenced by the intellects He created, rather than the absolute Architect of the cosmos. True prayer brings the Christian's will into conformity with that of the Enemy, who somehow managed within Himself to say, "Thy will be done in earth, as it is in heaven." Realistically speaking, from the vantage point of hell, we know that this is all some kind of theatrical performance on His part. He can't really "love" these misbegotten human hybrids, since they have nothing worthwhile to give Him in return. If "love" exists at all, it must somehow be practical and profitable. Someone somewhere must exploit somebody, and since He created them it follows that in the end this is His game.

Your patient must never learn about these things, so please, for your own benefit, pay attention to business. As you well know, the inexorable law of hell is that you either provide food or become food, and in your case for the present at least, the prospects are somewhat less than bright.

Your affectionate uncle,
SCREWTAPE

Letter XX

My Dear Wormwood:

You have hit upon a most important subject which, despite the brevity of your report, indicates that at last you are thinking instead of reacting. It is indeed galling that your patient's wife persuaded him to attend that sickening series of lectures dealing with basic conflicts in the home. They unfortunately enunciated the fact that the Enemy does indeed maintain a chain of command in His dealings with the humans, and specifically in regard to the life of His church. The reestablishment of domestic tranquility, not to mention the prayer life, of your patient and his wife constitutes a real setback, but there are still opportunities for you to recoup your losses.

You mentioned that your patient spends a great deal of time putting off till tomorrow what he can do for the Enemy today. This is a real opening. One of the humans has written that "procrastination is the thief of time." How true this is, and how well we have used this knowledge over the centuries. There is not the slightest doubt in my mind that untold damage has been done to the Enemy's cause, not so much by aborting His efforts (something which is becoming increasingly more difficult to accomplish) but by hindering His disciples from carrying out their appointed tasks through procrastination.

You mentioned that he has been stirred recently on the subject of Christian stewardship, or meeting the expenses of proclaiming the Enemy's message. He doubtless has been challenged by some crusading twit of a pastor to set apart a portion of his income in what the Enemy's Training Manual describes as a "tithe." You must expend every effort to see that he procrastinates where this decision is concerned, because if he ever begins to give systematically as the Enemy intends, he will not only advance that kingdom but cause the Enemy to bless him more abundantly than he has ever experienced in the past. This appears to be the heavenly rule of thumb, so to speak, and any fool can see if he has any perception whatever that the creature cannot exhaust the resources of the Creator. Admittedly, it is an impossibility to outgive Him, but your patient is not aware of this as yet and you must be careful that he remains in ignorance of it. There are many ways to procrastinate relative to the systematic support of the Enemy's work, and high on the list of objections that you must encounter him with is the charge of "legalism." This position is generally taken by those members of the Enemy's church who are attempting to have their cake and eat it too. We have labored long to encourage their reasoning in this area and to convince them that under the Enemy's "new" covenant His grace eliminates all responsibility to give Him ten percent of their earnings. Be sure to put him in contact with those members of his congregation who are adamant in their assertion that he is "no longer under law but under grace."

This is a useful phrase when removed from its context, because it conveys the totally erroneous impression that, because the Enemy redeems by grace, there is no longer any responsibility to divine law. Such persons harp continuously (under our careful supervision, to be sure) that you should not let your left hand know what your right hand is doing, and that the "old" covenant has been totally done away with in the new. Such asininity is valuable to us and on the surface appears plausible, as long as you take it literally. But taken in the sense that the Enemy intended, the left hand and right hand refer to an *attitude* of giving, which He requires to be in a totally altruistic framework. Between His law and His grace, then, there is in His mind no conflict, since the latter fulfills the former and does not abrogate it.

It is perfectly true that they do not *owe* the Enemy ten percent of anything by law, but if in His scheme they truly love Him (a fatuous concept at best), they will be forced to admit that they owe Him everything. Their obligation is not ten percent but one hundred percent, since He insists that they are not their own any longer but have been purchased with a price. How well we know that the letter of the law kills, but the Enemy maintains that His Spirit gives life, and He establishes the validity of His law by the sovereignty of His grace. I am sure your patient can be led to other members of his church who will maintain vigorously that systematic giving is not mentioned by name in the newer section of the Enemy's Training Manual. Of course they are perfectly correct, but if they would ever stop to think, it is a bankrupt argument at best. We here in hell all know that an argument from silence does not always fall by its own weight.

It could be pointed out to them (if anyone ever stopped to analyze it, which they don't) that the doctrine involving the threefold nature of the Enemy's Being is not itself mentioned by name in the same volume, yet they all faithfully maintain that *it* is true! It escapes them entirely that identical reasoning is involved in both cases, the first to deny and the other to affirm equally true propositions. No matter—we are not interested in their twisted thought processes; we are only interested in seeing that they procrastinate in supporting with their substance the Enemy's kingdom outreach, for in so doing they promote our ends and hinder His.

If you should fail to deter him by the methods so far outlined, steer him into that slough of spiritual despond known as compromise. We have had great successes with this approach. One case, notably chronicled in the Enemy's own Training Manual, involved a man and his wife who acknowledged that the Enemy was entitled to something for His trouble and attempted to negotiate a division of their assets with Him. On the reasonable thesis that their material possessions were their own and could be disposed of in any way that they saw fit, they withheld some of the funds due Him. The Enemy took an extremely unreasonable view of the entire proceedings, and their swift demise is a matter of record that His church never ceases to preach about.° Apparently His concept of giving involves the selfish notion that He owns the earth and everything in it. But, as our Father has said, it may be His by creation but it is ours by squatter's rights, and we mean to rule it— about that you may be certain there will be no procrastination.

In passing, it might be worth mentioning that, should your patient begin to systematically tithe, you must have him notice that the family budget will have to undergo radical revision if he is to be faithful. This generally results in a lack of enthusiasm when the humans perceive that they have given up their bird in the hand for the two in the bush promised by the Enemy. If this fails to discourage your patient, distract him with numerous other projects outside his local congregation, which in themselves are quite

---

° *Screwtape probably refers here to the fifth chapter of Acts.*

worthy of his support but which will diminish his giving to the local church. This will curtail its effectiveness to minister, and in the very area where he is the chief beneficiary. Encourage him to entertain every shortsighted view possible; never let him learn that the Enemy provides not only day by day but as the needs of the future present themselves. All of these arguments, approaches, methods, or tactics are designed to encourage procrastination on his part, and if you persevere they can bear much corrupt fruit for us.

There is one portion in the newer section of the Enemy's Training Manual which you must not allow him to peruse. In that portion the Enemy laid down the principle of giving on a grand scale and utterly demolished all arguments to the contrary, a most annoying habit He consistently practices. This section, using the older part of the Manual as a point of reference, reveals that the first Jew, Abraham (of unlamented memory), knelt before the Enemy's priesthood and paid his tithe to its high priest, Melchizedek. He then proceeds to point out that, when the Enemy appeared in the form of the humans, He too claimed that priesthood as an inviolate and untransferable order. This may all seem very academic, but it does make a startling and valid point you must obscure from your patient's view. Since Abraham paid tithe to that priesthood, and Abraham is designated the father of all true believers (in the spiritual sense, of course), then all believers owe tithe to that priesthood. That fact bridges the gap between His older and newer Training Manuals, annihilates the law-grace argument, and mandates a continuing tithe of faith. There is really no way out of it from this point of view, and if your patient once grasps this the Enemy's so-called royal law will stand clearly revealed. He will see his obligation and probably cheerfully respond, not because of law but because of the Enemy's grace.

You have no idea, Wormwood, how formidable

systematic giving on the part of Christians can be, and if they ever learn the truth about the whole matter, all of our carefully laid strategems will be swept away in a flood of hilarious benevolence. This we must not permit to happen, so help him procrastinate, not only in giving to the Enemy's work, but in every area connected with his Christian life. Promote, therefore, procrastination in his involvement with Christian missions, lay evangelism, local businessmen's groups, and, above all else, Christian laymen who distribute the Enemy's Training Manual on a massive scale and insist on carrying His message into their business life independent of the local church. They are the most dangerous because they are zealous, and he must avoid them at all costs.

The home is still another excellent place to practice procrastination, not only about normal duties connected with its maintainance but in the all-important zone of his wife and children. I note that he has been procrastinating for some time about having a family night where everyone can share experiences together. Such a time would emphasize not only prayer but practical application of their Christian ethic, such as painting the church or parsonage, visiting the infirm and the aged, or just staying home together. See that something always comes up to prevent this, and make it look legitimate.

He has also procrastinated about a family vacation and attendance at prayer meeting with his wife. His neighbor across the street can be helpful to you here because he is forever complaining that the church is encroaching upon his social life and has "something going every night." Now there's a man who can accelerate procrastination! What a pity that your patient cannot see that he does nothing for the Enemy's work except criticize those who promote it, and to that degree he is useful to us. I could go on at some length on this subject, but I think you grasp the significance of the whole picture. Procrastination is a progressively deteriorating practice that gradually numbs the spiritual senses and blinds the minds of those who do not detect that we are among its most avid promoters. The humans have not yet learned that whatever it is, whatever form it takes, or whatever motivation of altruism it may advance, anything that is interposed between them and the will of the Enemy for their lives is by definition connected with us and their own degenerate nature. Need I say that procrastination is the capstone on the whole pyramid of our demonic endeavors?

While you are about it, though, see that you get your next report in on time or the Council may come to the conclusion that somebody else is procrastinating besides your patient. Should that be the case, I need not warn you of the culinary consequences.

Your affectionate uncle,
SCREWTAPE

Letter XXI

My Dear Wormwood:

I am greatly encouraged by your last letter and was happy to learn that on both the domestic and business fronts your patient's faith is suffering substantial damage. I particularly enjoyed your comments on the effects of jealously and envy as they apply to his daily activities. The competition he is experiencing on the job from a younger and more highly educated rival must be fanned from the spark that it now is into a raging inferno of jealous antagonism. The Enemy will, of course, resist this effort on your part, since He considers both envy and jealousy to be "works of the flesh," indicative of carnality and devoid of spiritual self-control. Since your patient views his rival as a threat to his job security (a baseless assumption in view of his ability and seniority), play upon his fears of being "phased out," as it cannot help but disrupt his capacity to concentrate, thus diminishing his productivity. His employers are certain to notice these effects, and any word that they might speak to him will, in his present frame of mind, be interpreted as an additional threat to his position. He already envies his imagined competitor—not only his youth and appearance, but the way he makes difficult tasks appear easy.

I would suggest that you further aggravate his anxieties by provoking his temper, particularly when his employers compliment his competitor and fail to acknowledge his own contributions. The young man he fancies as his replacement actually knows nothing of his real feelings, so the more curt answers and gruff dialogue you can arrange for him to receive from your patient, the greater the tension between them will increase, so that what is now tolerance on his part can be handily converted to hate. Along with envy, be sure to introduce a generous mixture of jealousy, and mind that you do not confuse the two, for there is a very real difference. One of the humans, after analyzing the Enemy's distinction between them, observed that the goal of envy is a desire to deprive another of what he possesses, whereas jealousy is a desire to possess the same thing for one's self. Either way, we can make good use of both of them, since they can generate highly charged feelings of vicious displeasure simply by the victim seeing or hearing of the prosperity or success of others. In dealing with your patient, bear in mind that jealousy is the antithesis of what the Enemy designates as "love"; therefore, your patient's obsession with jealous feelings further serves to place him outside the sphere of grace and squarely in the center of what must be certain chastisement.

Down through the ages our experience with the humans has led us to conclude that they more often than not cut off their noses to spite their faces, and nothing removes a spiritual nose more rapidly than an envious heart and a jealous mind. Whatever you do, keep your patient from the knowledge that envy is as cruel as the grave, and that no one can successfully stand in its presence, for it consumes both subject and object before it is finished. Envy and jealousy can be either created or stimulated almost anywhere, with extraordinary results in most cases. For example, politicians frequently envy their colleagues the publicity they obtain from the various media, while some clergymen envy the pulpit success of their peers. The aging actor or actress envies the talent of his or her youthful contemporaries, while physicians and lawyers, housewives and athletes alike fall victim to the same emotion. Envy, then, is the mother of spiritual deterioration, and jealousy is her willing handmaiden.

One of the great by-products of both of these twin sisters of destruction is loneliness, that great forerunner of depression and terminal despair. It is strange but nonetheless quite true that with all the advancements of technology and the accelerated development of civilization over the last two centuries, the humans, despite their rapid multiplication, are more lonely now than at any other time in their history. It is no wonder that we have had such great success in promoting cultic and occultic religious phenomena; men will try anything to escape loneliness and boredom in an age characterized by both. The jealous or envious person must constantly turn inward to avoid an outward expression of his inner hostilities, and it is into this vacuum of the human spirit that some of our most successful ventures have been launched. The envy which seethes in your patient's soul will tend to make him remote from his colleagues at work and from his family at home. Give him every reason to feed upon any unpleasant experiences that will justify his feelings, and it will touch every corner of his life.

The Enemy, I might add, is not likely to permit any activity on your part for too long a period, so time (which He selfishly controls as a virtual monopoly) must not be wasted.

On the home front, your patient's wife can also fall victim to envy if you can shift her attention from her children and her church long enough for her to notice that many of her friends and neighbors are better housed, dressed, and otherwise materially benefited than she. Be certain that you do not cultivate her envy and its resultant jealousy solely on the basis of her own emotions. She is the kind that must be led into the practice of envy while still convinced that her feelings are altruistic at heart. Thus she will become jealous for her husband's success and jealous for her children's position in the community. In fact, let her be jealous *for* the benefit of anything and anybody, but do not let her guess that she is really envious and jealous *about* the success of others, which, of course, is the root of the entire matter.

One of the interesting things that our Father has pointed out on a number of occasions where the humans are concerned is the fact that they never connect envy and jealousy with its inevitable consequence—hate. Those who are dominated by jealousy and envy invariable become unconscious haters, though they would deny it vigorously if the accusation were made. Nevertheless, that is how it ends up, and you would be surprised at how many people are now occupying quarters in our Father's house because they failed to realize where their envious and jealous feelings were leading them.

Hatred is another subject which ought to be explored more thoroughly if we had the time, but there are different varieties of it just as there are different varieties of envy and jealousy. For instance, there are racial hatred, political hatred, economic hatred, and, the most rewarding of them all, religious hatred. The last variety has filled more space in hell than you could ever dream of. It is a real encouragement for us here to see thousands of rabid and pharisaical devotees of world religions still roundly denouncing each other in a symphony of unreconciled "pure hatred." Ah, for the bad old days, when the Enemy's servants persecuted, tortured, and murdered each other, all in the righteous name of "orthodoxy" and purity of doctrine. If we could only persuade them once again to crusade after one or another kind of "holy grail," what lavish repetitions of religious butchery we would revel in once more!

This particular area, incidentally, is always ripe for exploitation, because the old argument that religion has killed more people than all wars is still accepted coin in the classrooms of secular education. If they only knew that the genuineness of a professed disciple of religion can only be measured by his fidelity to the teachings of the founder of that particular religion, and not by his own excesses of zeal, the whole delusion would be unmasked forever. You may have opportunity to try this on your patient, particularly when he is trying to convert some of his skeptical and agnostic friends. Believe me, at the right moment it can be the perfect squelch. Should he find out, however, that the philosophies of Nazism and Communism have succeeded in murdering more persons in the last six decades than all the religious wars of recorded history have managed in more than five thousand years, our fat will quite literally be in the fire!

The Enemy's overall plan to combat these three deadly practices involves His tired old tactic of "love." He drives home his point quite forcefully, however, all too many times for our liking, demanding as He does that those who seek His forgiveness must first forgive others themselves. You must realize that if forgiveness for real or imagined grievances is extended to your patient's rival, the Enemy will in turn forgive him, so that all your work will be for nothing. If his mincing, disgustingly submissive wife discovers that the Enemy's "love" does indeed cover a multitude of sins, she too will escape our snare. By Lucifer, how I hate that love! Someday we will accumulate enough data to show the whole universe what fools He is making of the humans with this pious pretense of concern for their well-being, but until then be wary of His not inconsiderable abilities. He is a wise devil, indeed, who preys upon the weaknesses of humanity and thereby enriches the diet of hell.

Your affectionate uncle,
SCREWTAPE

Letter XXII

My Dear Wormwood:

It occurs to me, after reviewing carefully your last report, that you have run into one of the most uncommon of all of the irritating traits the two-legged rodents possess. I refer, of course, to persistence.

Your patient appears to have survived the onslaughts of envy and jealousy, and both he and his wife have avoided the trap of hatred by a direct intervention on the part of the Enemy's Spirit. There is no doubt about the fact that some humans have the capacity to persevere in the face of even the most gifted of tempters. Such specimens fortunately are few and far between, and I assure you, a little more homework on your part should serve to tip the scales in our favor.

One of the surest ways to discourage persistence is to confuse it in the minds of the humans with unattainable invincibility. Though it is true that persistence on the part of the Christian can hamper and at times totally disrupt our best efforts, it has a number of limitations, among which is susceptibility to diversion. The Enemy's Training Manual is replete with instances of how some of the most persistent characters in religious history were diverted from their appointed paths by ostensibly valid reasons. David of Israel, for example, persisted in his dream to build a house for the Enemy, only to have it snatched from his hand and bestowed upon another. In his case the diversionary tactic was Bathsheba in a bathtub. Another of the Enemy's choice servants, Moses by name, doggedly persisted in serving Him even at an advanced age, and led the rabble of Semitic slavery to the very borders of a promised land. He too was diverted from his ultimate goal by presumptuous anger that struck a rock and simultaneously struck down his entrance into Canaan. Samson was diverted by Delilah, Noah by wine, Elijah by fear. It bears repetition, as one of the humans has put it, that nothing can take the place of persistence. Wealth, education, talent, genius, and power will not—indeed cannot—be a substitute for persistence. Since it is encouraged in the character of the humans by the Enemy, we must divert them from employing it and discourage them from its application at every opportunity.

I have found that Christians can best be diverted from the performance of the Enemy's will for their lives by presenting them with various options to do good elsewhere. One of our more spectacular achievements in this field was realized when we persuaded a world-famous ecclesiastical figure that he could "reform" and "revitalize" an old-line denominational group by joining forces with them, rather than remaining an independent voice for the Enemy. We wooed him with educational kudos and gave him the prestige of a national radio and television audience while carefully exposing him to liberal theologians who quickly sterilized a large segment of his faith in the Enemy's Word, thereby robbing him of his zeal and power.

The Enemy's Spirit stubbornly refused to crown his preaching efforts with the trail of converts he had once known, but we were not to be denied. Large audiences still came to hear him, but they soon dwindled when he could no longer feed the spiritual famine in their souls. He was a handsome man with great gifts, and I shudder to think what he would have done to our Father's kingdom had we not discouraged his initial persistence. We did not hesitate, I might add, to use his own physical attributes to further drain off his already depleted spiritual resources. Women found him irresistible, and we in turn saw to it that he returned the compliment. Before long his marriage disintegrated, he became disenchanted with his denomination (which no longer had any real use for him), and today he is but a forgotten name, toiling in the secular world he once so persistently criticized.

In his case a combination of distracting factors brought him down, but none so decisively as his failure to persist in doing the Enemy's will.

If you are to have this type of success with your patient, you must undercut his persistence. Our records are filled with positive proof that humans are, by and large, far too lazy to persist in anything except the gratification of their own appetites and lusts. Those who do have the trait in any marked degree can pretty generally be misled by priorities that we carefully rearrange. Ambitious businessmen, for instance, can be kept so busy that they are unable to persist in the discipline of their children at home or in the proper management of their time in the office. We clutter their calendars with impossible schedules and persuade them to neglect their rest and diet in the pursuit of what we call "duty." They never pause to ask themselves what would happen if they were taken ill and could not perform what now seems to be so vitally important. Many of them soon find out the answer to this while looking up at the ceiling in an intensive care unit at the hospital. There are not a few ministers of the Enemy's gospel we have helped along the same route, only in their cases the diversionary tactic was somewhat different. We urged them, out of a false sense of piety and responsibility, to undertake more speaking engagements, writing assignments, and social functions than any six persons could normally perform, and to excuse their fatigue as "part of the price of serving the Lord." The Enemy quite naturally resents our misrepresentation in this area of His domain, but so far He has been powerless to prevent our filling large numbers of hospital beds and not a few cemetery plots with the splendid evidence of our ever-mounting success.

It's a good thing for us that they never get around to checking out the Enemy's Training Manual (volume 16:6) or all would be lost. In the instance there chronicled we lost out to the persistence of a man who simply would not come down off the walls of Jerusalem until he had finished the task the Enemy gave him to do. We gave him every legitimate reason we could think of, but he flung in our teeth the Enemy's dictum "Build the walls," and he persisted with maniacal fury to its completion. You see, our task is to get people off their several walls where the Enemy has placed them to accomplish His purposes. To that end we must utilize every deception and cunning to which hell is heir. Distract them with the legitimate, promote guilt over imaginary avoidance of duty, and above all divert the energy of persistence into any area, whether selfishness and greed or the highest principles of charity. Just don't, under any circumstances, permit your patient to persist in accomplishing the one priority, whatever it may be, that the Enemy has instructed him to perform.

Let me be most explicit about this, dear boy, as I sense a foreboding in the increased persistence of your patient's behavior pattern. You must take, if necessary, extreme measures, lest it become an overpowering habit. Should this unhappy circumstance prevail, his perseverance and obedience to the Enemy's will can cause him to become rooted and grounded in his faith, emerging at last as a most formidable foe of all we stand for. Prevent him at all costs from putting on the dread armor of the Enemy's army, for its shield is impenetrable and its sword terrible to feel. Even our Father, for all his fantastic abilities and devious cunning, hesitates to approach those who have appropriated the whole armor of the Enemy, because such maturity indicates power and determination to resist us in great strength. It is vital that your patient's persistence not culminate in such a terrifying encounter, and I am confident that you will do your duty to see that this never occurs. Let me encourage you once more to redouble your efforts, and, should you need any assistance, be assured that the complete resources of my department will be assembled in your behalf. All hell salutes you in the great common cause of making hell on earth.

Your affectionate uncle,
SCREWTAPE

Letter XXIII

My Very Dear Wormwood:

I am not in the least interested in your pitiful, inept excuses and your groveling attempts to patronize me. By all that's unholy, you have bungled it again! You've let the Enemy rescue another soul from the flames, and what a tasty morsel he would have made but for your sheer negligence. My sole consolation in the midst of this horrendous heavenly humiliation is the knowledge that at long last I shall be able to even the score with you. Hell hungers for the taste of lost souls, but in their absence we have not hesitated to sample and even relish clumsy tempters such as yourself. Once more you have somehow managed to snatch defeat from the jaws of victory. Beelzebub, if you haven't got your nerve even asking for a review of the case before we can deal with you! It is seducing spirits such as you that give our college and training facilities a good name in the Enemy's realm; in fact, you are at moments like this probably one of the best (and hopefully unwilling) allies that He has!

There is no need to prolong disucssion of this subject;

you may rest assured that the Hades High Council will give you what justice you richly deserve, and we all await your arrival with increasingly ravenous appetites.

Please do not burden me any further with lengthy descriptions of what transpired at the moment your patient was released through death from the disintegrating confines of what the Enemy refers to as His supreme earthly achievement—the human body. By Lucifer, it is humiliating to see creatures created a little lower than the angels and during their earthly lifespan subjected to disease, privation, suffering, and even the indignities of temptation from both their carnal natures and our sustained activities, suddenly and in a moment claiming their inheritance as sons of the Enemy. Did you not notice as he approached the moment of death how easily and almost naturally he called upon the Enemy in prayer? Did you not sense the suffocating and awesome presence of that alien Spirit, who somehow manages to always appear at the moment of our expected triumph and dash the fondest hopes of hell upon the rock of inflexible grace?

No, I have not forgotten how the humans fear death, but neither has the Enemy, and to see Him suddenly appear, that eternal Shepherd of their souls, who openly thwarted our Father's best efforts on a Roman cross, is more than even the most powerful and conditioned tempter can bear to look upon. He has promised to lead them through the valley of the shadow of death, which indeed, despite our best efforts, has become just that—a shadow instantaneously dispersed as if by the brillance of a billion galaxies. I tell you, it is more than I can bear to recollect. Quite apart from your insipid whinings, I know that from the onset of the heart attack he suffered so suddenly to the moment of his death, you had very little time to terrify him sufficiently, so that fear, which indeed torments, could have produced doubt and the conviction that the Enemy had abandoned him.

But you missed your great moment of opportunity when one of our faithful hirelings, the hospital chaplain, undercut the entire structure of the Enemy's message by telling him that all religions were of equal value and that the Enemy, who is "a God of love," would not think of sending anyone to eternal hell. You should have used this to capitalize upon his condition of weakness and thereby lull him into a false sense of security and a trust in his own good works. However, with your usual talent for neglect of detail, you permitted his wife to read to him from the Enemy's Training Manual—a maddening experience in frustration—thereby reinforcing his faith in the Enemy's capacity to forgive and, upon confession, to cleanse him of all sin. I can feel even now the biting, excruciating thrusts of what the Enemy calls "the Sword of the Spirit." How you must have recoiled as again and again you were skewered by the burning penetration of terrifying truths. At times the words she read to him, amplified by the Enemy's Spirit, reverberated down the very corridors of hell itself, causing even our Father below to feel the shuddering impact of the Enemy's victory.

How I wish our Intelligence Department would conceive of a methodology to bind the Enemy's Word and effectively resist His Spirit. Did you not see how your patient reveled in the comfort of the Enemy's promises? "Death," He tells them, is "to be swallowed up by life." Because "He lives," they will live also, and that to be absent from the body is to be in His very presence. Were you not aware that at that moment all our efforts crumbled to ashes? He knew us for what we are, but far more than this he at last was free of us, and all our efforts were lost. Formed from the dust of the earth though he was, the Enemy's breath set him apart from all creation. His body will return to the dust from whence it came, but at that moment he knew that his spirit would return to the One who gave it. What joy he knew at that moment, and what untold suffering and agony you felt in your being. The anchor of his body had been weighed.

The tent in which he lived was struck down, and all we were left with was what the Enemy promised our Father long ago in Eden—a mouthful of dust! How humiliating for spirits of our magnitude to experience the degradation of the Enemy's triumph. What heavenly nausea crept over you as He spoke—"well done, good and faithful servant; enter into the joy of thy Lord." Of course we know there is no real joy, that somehow or other He is planning to exploit them with what He refers to as His "love," and that despite this victory it is only one of many battles. In the end, by hell, we will win the invisible war. But none of the things you saw, Wormwood, will ever be erased from your memory, for the Enemy has one final humiliation in store for us. He has promised that even our mouthful of dust will become an eternal mockery of our impotence to thwart His will. This obscenity He calls the resurrection, when the corruption we now have as dust will become incorruption, and the mortal we have tempted and tormented will become immortality. Death will have lost its sting and the grave its illusory victory. He intends no less than that death itself, their greatest fear as mortals, will through the resurrection be swallowed up by immortal life.

He has promised them that they shall be like Him. They shall actually see Him as He is. Of course our Father knows Him for what He is, and we have his absolute word that it is all hypocracy. But nonetheless your rapid exit from the upward ascent of his soul, coupled with the expressions of joy and praise emitting from the heavenly choirs, chokes one with the noxious fumes of an environment which only a submissive, subservient fool could find acceptable.

I confess, alas, that despite the truthfulness of our observation, the creatures do appear to enter the Enemy's presence with a type of emotion peculiar to His own nature. I believe He describes it as a peace the world cannot give.

But never fear. Someday our Department of Devilish Intelligence will succeed in penetrating His long-range defensive system, and we will have access to what really makes Him what He is. It is then that we will discover the source of His frustrating power. In the face of what sometimes appears to be our certain defeat, I am sustained by the overriding conviction that He possesses an intellect without discipline and power without a real or enduring purpose. True reality must therefore lie with our Father below, who will one day lead us in that successful invasion of the Enemy's realm that will forever overthrow His unrealistic and weak capacities to deal with creation. In the words of a human who was foolish enough to endorse our Father's philosophy, we are the captains of our fate; we are the masters of our souls. Everything else is heavenly nonsense.

In the meantime, beloved and anticipated morsel, the famine of hell cries out for you, none of which is more famished than

> Your affectionate uncle,
> SCREWTAPE

Epilogue

Memo to: Undersecretary Screwtape, T.E., B.S., etc.

From: His Abysmal Excellency, Dragonslik, D.S.T.°
Director, Division of Devilish Intelligence,
Defender of the Faithless

My Dear Screwtape:

I am delighted at your contemplated return to active service. I am certain that your "vacation" at D.R.C.°° (albeit enforced) has been of real assistance to you in reappraising and rearranging your priorities as a Supervisional Tempter. I regret sincerely the misunderstanding you had with my nephew, Wormwood, and we will forget, for the present at least, your attempt to have him served as the main course at the annual banquet of young tempters at Slubgob's College! He may indeed be, as you suggested, a "tasty morsel," but I will determine who feasts on whom and when. Incidentally, Slubgob assures me that he tried to dissuade you from this foolhardy path but that you rashly insisted. I hope you have learned your lesson from this. Remember, even hell has its chain of command, and by forgetting this and in your zeal to devour Wormwood, you made our admittedly unpleasant disciplinary measures necessary.

° *Doctor of Satanic Tactics*
°° *Devilish Rehabilitation Center*

Rest assured, however, that your record remains relatively unblemished despite this indiscretion, for we feel that you have many evil centuries of service left in our Father's kingdom. Try, if you can, to remember that you are to *teach* young fiends that profane science and methodology of temptation—*discipline* is our affair, and if you dare to forget it again, you will . . . !

But that is not relevant to our present goals, so put it out of your mind.

I personally think you have done a commendable job on the whole where many immature demons are concerned, and your Alice in Wonderland approach (through the looking glass or the pernicious redefinition of terms found in the Enemy's Training Manual) can only be termed brilliant. We here at D.D.I. are confident that your future counsel and advice to junior tempters will increase the evil effectiveness of their many contemplated (but as yet unrealized) sorties into the Enemy's realm.

Glory to Lucifer in the lowest!

DRAGONSLIK